SOCIALISMS

REVISITING REVOLUTIONS BETRAYED, MISLAID AND UNMADE

SOCIALISMS

REVISITING REVOLUTIONS BETRAYED, MISLAID AND UNMADE

Ian Parker

Resistance Books
IIRE

Socialisms: Revisiting Revolutions Betrayed, Mislaid and Unmade is issue number 66 of the IIRE Notebooks for Study and Research

© Ian Parker

Cover design by Ben Beechey

ISBN: 978-0-902869-71-4

Published 2020 by Resistance Books, London and the IIRE, Amsterdam

For the intrepid inquisitive travellers
present at various different points in this text
where I refer to 'we' or 'us':
Adam, Alpesh, Ana-Cris, Berenice, Chris, David
and, of course, Erica

CONTENTS

Introduction: Blueprints   1

1. Russian Federation   7
2. Georgia   29
3. Republic of Serbia   47
4. Democratic People's Republic of Korea   65
5. People's Republic of China   91
6. Republic of Cuba   119
7. Lao People's Democratic Republic   145
8. Bolivarian Republic of Venezuela   159

Bibliography   181

About Resistance Books and the IIRE   185

INTRODUCTION

BLUEPRINTS

This book provides accessible description and assessment of attempts to transcend capitalism in Europe, Asia and Latin America. It combines an account of travel in eight countries that have experienced some form of socialist transformation with historical analysis of what happened and what went wrong. The eight countries under examination here – Russia, Georgia, Serbia, China, North Korea, Laos, Cuba and Venezuela – went through the process of revolt against capitalism in very different ways, and the failure to build socialism in each separate case offers many lessons for those who still rebel against exploitation and oppression and who want a better world.

I make no pretence to get 'back-stage' and to directly see what these countries are really like in this book. Such direct empirical visible data is not actually only the stuff of Marxism at any rate; Marxism is a method of analysis which focuses on underlying political-economic processes, and for that you need historical context and an attention to the fault-lines in a social system which themselves become evident over time, evident in conscious collective attempts to change the world. I have set out some of the compass points for that kind of analysis, and you need to read my anecdotal observations against that background, a background that I flesh out in the course of this book.

There was no blueprint for socialism in the 1848 *Communist Manifesto,* and both Marx and Engels, along with most revolutionaries seeking an overthrow of capitalist society, have wisely avoided spelling out exactly how a socialist society would be organised. Marx's own suggestion, in his 1875 *Critique of the Gotha Programme,* that post-capitalist society might travel through 'socialist' and then 'communist' stages of development offered a poisoned chalice to revolutionary leaders seeking to justify the necessarily limited steps they were taking in a hostile world. This, and the claim that it would indeed be possible to build 'socialism in one country' while under attack from the rest of the capitalist world, was then combined by Stalinist apologists for the bureaucratic suppression of democracy in each country they controlled with the idea that there were strict 'stages' of development of society. It would then be possible, they argue, to understand and justify the limitations of actually-existing socialist societies with reference to the linear path of history from slavery to feudalism to capitalism and, only after that, to socialism.

The experience of the attempt to build socialism in each of the eight countries described in this book speaks against those claims. These revolutions broke from the linear 'stage' model of political-economic development derived from a misreading of Marx, and they each, in their own particular way, valiantly attempted to strike out on a different path which would replace individual ownership and control of the means of production – 'the dictatorship of the bourgeoisie' – with collective ownership. This book describes how it was in and part of each separate revolutionary process that revolutionary Marxists insisted that the so-called 'dictatorship of the proletariat' must, in Lenin's words, be by definition 'a thousand times more democratic' than capitalism, and such an argument was eventually codified in Ernest Mandel's 1985 document written for the Fourth International *Dictatorship of the Proletariat and Socialist Democracy*, and later extended by perspectives on women's liberation and on ecosocialism in what Catherine Samary terms 'decolonial communism'.

Revolutionary Marxists have avoided setting out a blueprint for socialism for at least three reasons, and the attempts to build 'socialism' explored in this book underline the importance of each of these reasons. The first is that our imagination about what socialism will look like is always conditioned and limited by the shape of present-day society. The exploitative and oppressive social relationships that make capitalist accumulation of profit by a limited few possible set a template for any alternative world we could conjure into existence. We kick against this miserable world, and we hope for something better, and that creative revolt opens up something new. A revolutionary break with capitalism then makes it possible, and it is only when we are released from the confines of class-hatred and the correlative forms of racism and sexism and systematic exclusion of those who are deemed 'unproductive' that we can really begin to imagine and enact something completely different.

The second reason why we avoid blueprints is that any particular present-day context is continually changing, mutating, and opening up false paths in which capitalism, which is the most fluid and innovative system of political-economic organisation that the world has ever seen, is able to adapt every proposed alternative to its own ends. Capitalism recuperates, absorbs and neutralises, each and every idea about change, and this means that every blueprint is susceptible to distortion such that progressive social programmes then became part of the problem instead of part of the solution.

The third reason is at the heart of the process of revolutionary change, a process we see sparks of in this book, sparks which are then difficult to keep burning and too-often extinguished. Socialism is not a blueprint to be handed down to people as if it were a technical solution to a problem of efficient social organisation. It is a process of self-organisation through which people learn through their own collective self-activity what is possible and discover ways to put their ideas into practice.

Each specific country operates as a particular combination of factors at play on a global scale. Complete independence of any nation state once capitalism took hold as a global system is an illusion, in some cases it is an unavoidable illusion that sustains national liberation struggles that then gives way to a process of building economic and political ties and international solidarity. That practical impossibility of socialism in one country – political-economic isolation – was accompanied by another kind of isolation, with deadly consequences.

The formation of the First, Second, Third and then Fourth Internationals was predicated on the revolutionary Marxist understanding that successful combat against capitalism and its eventual overthrow depended on the accumulation of experiences from diverse parts of the world, from parts of the working class and from among its allies. Anti-capitalist struggle is complemented and enriched by the experience of anti-colonial movements, anti-racist movements, and by women's liberation and sexual liberation, ecological struggle and other dimensions of resistance against exploitation and oppression. Such heterogeneous complex political experiences must be drawn from across the globe so the working class itself can come to realise in its own practice the way in which its specific circumstances are intertwined with the operation of those multiple elements on an international level.

These eight attempts to build socialism in three very different parts of the world are testimony to the resistant energy and hope of people to escape from the confines of capitalism and find a better way to organise society, organise it for themselves rather than for the rich and powerful. What is amazing about these places where there was an attempt to build socialism is not that they failed but that there was a concerted struggle to go beyond capitalism. They failed, and we must learn from those failures, precisely in order that we might better succeed in the future. That guiding principle in this sympathetic examination of forms of socialism through a revolutionary Marxist lens is one grounded in solidarity with those who dared, and solidarity with those who are still steadfast in refusing what capitalism offers.

1

RUSSIAN FEDERATION

We begin in 1917 with a ground-breaking attempt to overthrow capitalism, a short-lived inspiring success that had consequences for the shape of other attempts around the world over the next century, and then failure, a return to full-blown capitalism with no-less dramatic consequences for socialists today.

The Russian Federation is the worst of capitalism reborn and triumphant from the ruins of the Soviet Union. The last head of state of the Soviet Union, Mikhail Gorbachev was in full command from 1988 until 1991 after becoming CPSU party secretary in 1985, overseeing the end of the Soviet project and the disintegration of the Union into a federation comprising twenty two supposedly independent republics. Judged by land-mass area Russia is the largest single country in the world. This 'federation' is still effectively ruled by Vladimir Putin from Moscow, a return to something very like the 'prison house of nations' that Lenin described shortly before the October 1917 Revolution, a revolution that finally overthrew the old Tsarist regime. The last three years of the Soviet Union under Gorbachev saw the foundations being laid for the capitalist economy and imperial ambition that Putin has presided over since his rise to power from within the security apparatus, the FSB, successor of the KGB.

Gorbachev's reforms had a double edge, cutting away on the one side against the old Stalinist bureaucracy in 'glasnost' – a new openness and transparency that saw a flourishing of social democratic and liberal ideas as well as some limited space for the re-emergence of authentic revolutionary Marxist debate – and destroying the economic foundations of what was left of the workers state in 'perestroika' which explicitly aimed to restructure society and return it to the global economy, return it to capitalism.

Gorbachev's period of rule saw the fall of the Berlin Wall in 1989 and its final destruction in November 1991, from the scrabble for consumer goods by those fleeing from the east in the 'soviet bloc' to the complete reintegration of Germany, and then the rest of Eastern Europe into the capitalist world.

The Soviet Union under Lenin from October 1917 to December 1991 was marked by the particular contradictions of a Russian Empire that housed a massive peasant population and a very small organised industrial working class – not at all the conditions that Marx described for socialist revolution to succeed – and then a civil war, during which there was invasion, sabotage and isolation by fourteen other capitalist nations whose ruling class feared that they would be next for the chop. This weak economic base and political demoralisation was fertile ground for Stalin to crystallise a bureaucracy that revived Great Russian sentiment as the ideological core of its 'peaceful coexistence' with imperialism.

It is little wonder that though it was in some sense 'post-capitalist', the Soviet Union was not, as it claimed, 'socialist', still less communist, and its systematically distorted vision of what socialism would be had dire consequences for radical movements for change around the world. The template it offered for an alternative to capitalism was authoritarian and corrupt, and Stalin imposed this template on the communist parties of the Third International, turning them from being instruments of struggle into instruments of the diplomatic needs of the bureaucracy.

Just as the character of the Soviet Union was marked by the contradictions of the society it negated, transformed and claimed to transcend, so the Russian Federation's political-economic system reflects the cocoon-regime it emerged from. If capitalism was supposed to have created the proletariat as the gravedigger of that historically obsolete system of rule, as Marx and Engels proposed in the 1848 *Communist Manifesto*, then the Putin regime has effectively turned the hopes of world revolution and global communism into the graveyard of socialism; the Russian Federation is one of the homes of zombie capitalism.

The Russian Federation has been functioning as an afterlife of capitalism. It is still, rather bizarrely, seen by some socialists as a progressive alternative after 1991, but it has shed even the symbolic pretence to be socialist. These are the remains of a revolution betrayed. This capitalist state will need to be dismantled in collective revolt, revolution, if the hopes of Lenin's October are ever to be rediscovered and put into practice.

Perestroika

So, in 1995, this is what capitalism looked like here. Gorbachev has gone, first and last President of the Soviet Union, a post created by himself as part of his swansong. We are nearly five years into the new dispensation under the first President of the Russian Federation, notorious drunk Boris Yeltsin, former member of the Communist Party of the Soviet Union, CPSU, now reborn as a neoliberal nationalist who steered the country to full-blown privatisation. Glasnost has given way to perestroika, which includes economic shock therapy, lifting of price controls and implementation of a market exchange rate for the rouble. Yeltsin is imposing a political-economic programme that had been recommended to Gorbachev by the International Monetary Fund. Millions of people have been plunged into poverty by these reforms, and state enterprises have been snapped up by the new oligarchs, mostly former prominent apparatchiks in the Soviet bureaucracy. There is capital flight, full economic depression, a fall in production, a fall in the birth rate and an increase in the death rate.

Hotel Cosmos in Moscow, still operated by Intourist, which was founded as a state travel agency in 1929 and privatized in 1992, is a 1,777-room curved gold-painted monstrosity built for the 1980 Olympics and now dumping point for foreign tourists who have to navigate their way through gaggles of prostitutes in the ground-floor lobby. While these women are selling their bodies to make a rouble inside the hotel, the end of the drive approach to the VDNKh Metro station is lined with little old wizened babushkas standing behind mats on which are arrayed a couple of even more wizened vegetables and batteries and other bits and pieces from their homes. They are desperately poor, offering what they have to visitors, barely surviving after the destruction of social services, depletion of pensions and rises in inflation and rent-prices. These are the bitter fruits of the betrayal of socialist revolution, so bitter that people are then also ripe for nationalist propaganda that is replacing the internationalist ethic of the Bolshevik Party and the Third International.

The revolution is also being sold off for very low prices in the flea-markets, with hat badges and medals and other memorabilia marketed as nostalgic tat, some of it fake; memories of a history of hopes for the future displayed as no more than unwanted detritus from the past. The Metro sure is ornate, as has been promised in the sightseeing tour itinerary, and so are the domes of the Russian Orthodox cathedrals, institutions given a new lease of life with the fall of the Wall and the rise of a form of capitalism that combines harsh realities about stock-exchange metrics with a new mysticism of the market and hopes for a life beyond it after death.

Lenin is long dead, his waxy-faced perpetually reconstructed stuffed body lit up for view in the mausoleum in Red Square, but viewed quickly; tourists are shuffled through after a quick glance at a revolutionary leader who made it very clear that he did not want to be embalmed or displayed as if he were a modern-day pharaoh. This is one more symbol of the decay of the revolution within ten years of October 1917. The revolutionary sequence of events which began with the February 1917 revolution and the seizure of power by Alexander Kerensky at the head of a liberal-democratic 'provisional government' signalled the end of Tsar Nicholas II, but not the end of Tsarism as such.

The rapid shift in power in October saw not only a shift of leadership from Kerensky as head of the provisional committee of the 'State Duma', or officially-recognised parliament, to Lenin as head of the Petrograd Soviet of Workers' and Soldiers' Deputies; it was a shift in the nature of power as such, from leaders to deputies, from authoritarian figures to the people, to workers and to soldiers who were also, of course, workers. The October Revolution was a world-historic event because though it was, indeed, led by Lenin and the Bolsheviks (the Communist Party and then CPSU), its dynamic and logic was to a deeper democratic mandate for the people, people from different nationalities taking collective control of their own lives through the 'soviets' as their representative assemblies.

That dynamic and logic was under pressure during the civil war and was finally stalled with the installation of Stalin as General Secretary of the Communist Party of the Soviet Union in 1922. It was Stalin who insisted that Lenin be turned into a dummy image of personal power and put in a mausoleum in Moscow because it was exactly that centralisation of power that Stalin desired and enacted himself. Lenin's body is a harsh reminder of something possible when he was alive and something deep-buried after he was dead. About a half-hour walk away is the first McDonalds in Moscow which opened in 1990, a message from Gorbachev to the West that Russia was open for business and a message to the Russian people that they had better move fast to make the best of it. Crowds flocked to the outlet, and queues stretched to buy fast food that would further boost already chronic obesity, though now, five years on, 1995, the lines of people are smaller and their pockets emptier. This is one of the symbols of the success of capitalism re-implanting itself in the country and of the poverty it feeds on.

There is an overnight train in 1995 from Moscow to Petrograd, the city that became Leningrad after the revolution but which is now renamed, ideologically returned to the Romanov Tsarist pre-revolutionary days as 'St Petersburg'. The little people with their power stripped away from them attempt to seize it back in petty displays of authority, and so it is on the train where each sleeper carriage is zealously managed by a scowling overweight guard who locks the toilets before every screeching juddering station-stop and then releases the occupants of the berths to relieve themselves in the dark when the train has got moving again.

Moscow is the present-day power-base of the bureaucrats in the Kremlin, the most important of the Russian fortresses which dominate cities around the federation, but it is revolutionary Petrograd that was the place where the transformation in 1917 really happened. This is where the Winter Palace, official residence of the Tsars and then site of the February 1917 provisional government, was stormed by Bolshevik Red Army soldiers and sailors, a defining moment of the October

Revolution. It is a revolution that is often represented as violent, a bloody combat engaged in by desperate men and women, but the really violent bloody days were to come much later and as a direct result of the White Army troops attempting to crush popular power, to take back control, to place it back in the hands of the large landowners, the agricultural and industrial ruling class. The Winter Palace in 1995 was a serene sight, the Hermitage art collection closed, and it was easier to appreciate that more people were killed during the reconstruction of the revolution in the 1920 Eisenstein film *October* than in the actual events it was designed to remind us of.

Hotel Astoria in St Petersburg opened in 1912, ready for tourists attending the Romanov tercentenary celebrations the following year, and it was patronised by the aristocracy, and apparently by Grigori (Rara) Rasputin, lover of the Russian queen, until the Bolsheviks came to power. Lenin spoke from the balcony in 1919, Mikhail Bulgakov was rumoured to have written part of *The Master and Margarita* in the hotel, and it was used as a field hospital during the siege of Leningrad in the Second World War. Rasputin was reputedly poisoned and shot and eventually dumped in the River Neva by aristocrats worried by the malign influence the monk had over members of the royal family.

The first issue of a free listings magazine *Pulse* had just hit the streets in 1995 proclaiming in one of its cover headlines that 'John Lennon Lives On'. Issue 2 of the *Neva News* in May 1995 devoted pages 3 and 4 to its 'Business Monitor' updates, and the 'Press Digest' on the back page had one article telling readers that Boris Yeltsin 'loves swimming in cold water. He is also a keen hunter and shoots ducks and wild board. He is a professional shot', and another article headed by a quote by Nikolai Ryzhkov, one of the directors of Tveruniversalbank, declaring that 'Gorbachev has no prospects'.

Matryoshka

I bought a set of wooden nested dolls from a market. The outermost one was of Boris Yeltsin, and emblazoned with the pre-1917 double-headed eagle of the Russian Empire. Next in was Mikhail Gorbachev, his belly marked with the letters CCCP (Russian Cyrillic script initials of the Union of Soviet Socialist Republics). Inside Gorbachev is Leonid Brezhnev, here wearing his army medals, an old bruiser who lasted from 1964 to 1982. That means some short-lived characters have been missed out. Yuri Andropov, a security apparatus thug was, earlier in his career, involved in the crushing of the Hungarian uprising of 1956 and the Prague Spring in 1968, and only lasted 15 months in power after Brezhnev. Konstantin Chernenko only lasted 13 months, and gave way to Gorbachev.

Who is this smaller guy nestling inside Brezhnev? It is Nikita Krushchev who ruled the roost from 1953 to 1964, a pretty key figure in the so-called 'de-Stalinisation' process. An ear of corn is smudged across his chest to signify his peasant origins. Georgy Malenkov had bridged the gap as de facto leader after Stalin, but was quickly edged aside, and it was Krushchev who took the reins of power, delivering a key report to the twentieth congress of the

CPSU in 1956 that attacked Stalin's 'cult of personality'. Krushchev made it seem as if that was the main problem and as if future leaders, including him, did not indulge in that kind of personality cult as much as they could get away with. And so, in this tracing back of the leadership of the party and nation, we come to a still smaller moustachioed wooden figure in army livery, Joseph Vissarionovich Stalin, the man of steel who held the USSR in his bloody grip from 1922 until his death in 1953.

Besuited Lenin is inside Stalin, not a nice metaphor, and, even more inaccurately, the last little piece is Tsar Nicholas II, the last of the Romanovs. Who did you expect to be at the inner core of the diminishing series in this historical chronology of state power? Leon Trotsky? Perhaps Trotsky could have been inside the Lenin matryoshka doll, animating strategy over the course of the revolution. Trotsky it was, after all, who had written the ground-breaking 1905 text on 'permanent revolution' which included the claim that Russia and other so-called 'backward' countries' were not doomed to repeat a strict linear schedule of development which led them from slavery to feudalism to capitalism and only then to socialism and communism. Globalisation of capitalism and the 'combined and uneven development' it unleashed meant that the revolutionary fate of each country was interdependently linked to the rest of the world.

This was not only a thoroughly internationalist conception of what Marx had been arguing, but one that brought the peasantry into the equation as agents of change acting alongside the industrial working class, the proletariat that had been called into being by capitalism.

16

Permanent revolution theorised in advance what actually took place in Russia in 1917 from February to October; Lenin implemented a quasi-Trotskyist political programme to make October possible. Socialist revolution was now on the cards everywhere in the world, but only if extended from Russia and acting independently of it. Lenin made it clear that the Soviet Union would only survive as a democratic socialist holding point if the revolution there spread, and that there could be no 'socialism in one country'.

If Trotsky was not to be the final piece of the puzzle inside Lenin, then why not place Lenin at the centre and have Trotsky as the next up, next in line? After tracing things back in time through the leadership of the party, we can trace things back again to the present day through the self-activity of the working class and the most authentic representatives of that process, the Trotskyists.

Lenin made it clear before he died in 1924 that Stalin was a bully and should not succeed him, and though he expressed doubts about the capabilities and sometimes arrogant character of Trotsky, his 'last testament' signalled that your man would have been the preferred choice. The Trotskyist continuation of the most democratic and revolutionary Marxist hopes of the October Revolution was expressed first through the 'Left Opposition', and then through a network of small groups that looked to Trotsky for guidance after he was sent into internal exile and then expelled from the Soviet Union by Stalin in 1929.

Trotsky was by no means perfect, and was, let's face it, directly implicated in the suppression of the workers' and sailors' revolt at Kronstadt in 1921, but the evolution of Trotskyism as a distinct political current, one that was then identified by Stalin as a main threat to his own power, went way beyond those personal failings. This political current became a historically-grounded defence of revolutionary Marxism as it pitted itself against the Stalinist bureaucracy and its crimes not only at home but also internationally. Trotskyists were murdered inside and outside the Soviet Union by Stalin's agents, and then finally Trotsky was felled in exile in Mexico in 1940, but not before he wrote his influential analysis of the regime *The Revolution Betrayed: What is the Soviet Union and Where is it Going?*, published in 1937. He founded the Fourth International in 1938 with a manifesto that included trade-mark Trotskyist 'transitional demands' which linked current concerns with the destruction of capitalist property and state structures that prevent basic socially progressive humanitarian measures being implemented. The so-called 'Transitional Programme' in the *Death Agony of Capitalism and the Tasks of the Fourth International* was effectively an update of the Communist Manifesto and a call to arms in the twentieth century.

The Fourth International, FI, had a big enough impact inside the Soviet Union, and more so outside it inside the Stalinised Third International Communist Parties around the world, to make the bureaucracy crack down hard; tiny though it was, it operated as a reminder of what the revolution should have been about. After Stalin's death, Krushchev's 1956 speech was given in a closed session of the CPSU, and so dramatic were the implications for communists around the world that copies had to be smuggled out. During the Krushchev and Brezhnev eras, activists from the FI were actively taking advantage of the small space opened up for debate, and the main demand of the FI was for more openness but no return to capitalism; 'for glasnost and against perestroika'. That is why the FI supported the rights of all Soviet and East European 'dissidents' whether or not they were self-declared socialists.

Glasnost

The following years, four years to the end of Yeltsin's bungled handling of the handover of assets to the new multi-millionaires – chaotic times that other Stalinist states like China have been keen to avoid as they busily privatise the economy – and then from 1999 onward under Putin, have seen more restructuring and less openness. Calendars and mugs on sale in the Metro underpass kiosks in Moscow in December 2013 sported manly Putin undressed to the waist riding horses or braving the torrents to fish. The freezing snow made me wish I had brought the prickly grey fur hat with me that I had picked up back in 1995.

Putin makes visible what was claimed for Yeltsin as the good hunter and crack-shot, and he has the left in his sights. Putin's restructuring of Russia as a full-blown capitalist state has two aspects that parody what the born-again social-democratic Gorbachev had seemed to offer: on the one hand, perestroika was reconfigured as the restructuring of the capitalist state as the most authoritarian of neoliberal experiments, combining the stripping back of social security and welfare with the imposition of state security and internal and external warfare; on the other hand, glasnost was reconfigured as a confused contradictory mélange of ideas that seem designed to ensure that Russians have no compass to work out what is going on and, as a consequence, distrust everything they are told. Two studies of these phenomena are especially useful.

Tony Wood's 2018 *Russia Without Putin: Money, Power and the Myths of the New Cold War* dismantles the first aspect, showing that the Putin regime is a direct continuation of Yeltsin's privatisation of state holdings, a process that began under Gorbachev. There is therefore nothing amazingly 'mafia-like' about Russian capitalism; it is operating as a neoliberal capitalist state and so comparable with the other capitalist states in the world it competes with. The book also then demonstrates that the so-called 'peaceful coexistence' that Brezhnev steered his way through from Krushchev continues, with an attempt by Putin not so much to engage in a great-power battle with the West but to participate in the scramble for spoils as an integral part of imperialism.

So, rather than being a break with the Stalinist past, the nature of capitalism in present-day Russia is very much shaped by those old bureaucratic managerial practices instituted under Stalin. Stalinist state-management was ripe for privatisation, and especially for the kind of privatisation and securitisation that characterises many other authoritarian neoliberal states around the world. Wood only briefly references Trotsky and *The Revolution Betrayed*. However, his argument is compatible with the 'decolonial communist' and revolutionary Marxist tradition that followers have attempted to keep alive outside Russia and then back inside it.

Peter Pomerantsev's 2014 *Nothing is True and Everything is Possible: Adventures in Modern Russia* is a less Trotskyist and more surreal journey through Putin's surreal ideological universe, mapping the media strategies that are used by the regime to bewitch and bemuse the population. The book begins with the exploitation and oppression of women, and the heteropatriarchal nature of contemporary capitalism is visible throughout. The contradictory ideological assault on reason backed up by pure force entails not only the revival of Russian Orthodox mysticism, but public dabbling in many other kinds of mystical and conspiratorial belief systems; raising possibilities, debunking them, pointing the finger at the West for peddling untruths and then implicitly subscribing to each and every one of them. This is the world of post-Soviet reality as a kind of simulacrum in which it matters not so much what lies behind the surface but efficiently functions to institute the suspicion that there are only surfaces and that it will be impossible to know the truth. This is a paranoid ideological universe which allows private interests to shape public discourse, particularly those private interests linked to Putin, and so it also feeds ridiculous and toxic conspiracy theories.

These are the ideological preconditions for alliances between what remains of the old Communist Party and extreme right-wing political agendas, of 'red-brown' politics. This fuels racism and the rise again of antisemitism, this in the land of the pre-revolutionary notorious faked conspiracy theory 'documents' and pogroms against Jews; conspiracy theories now also often saturated with Islamophobia.

Putin's Russia is not only zombie capitalism but also 'Zombie Stalinism'. It entails a significant rewriting of history, one in which Lenin is now viewed as a threat, increasingly 'criminalised' retroactively by the regime, and in which ecological, feminist and socialist activists in the anarchist and Trotskyist groups are targeted. There are even state-media tolerated hints that Lenin himself may have had Jewish blood, and this, of course, then also means that Leon Trotsky is completely beyond the pale. The limited opening after Gorbachev did enable the formation of activist groups that eventually, in a politically significant development, led to the formation, after many years absence, of a Russian section of the Fourth International called 'Vpered' (Forward) in 2010, and then, a year later, its fusion with other forces to form the present-day Russian Socialist Movement.

In 2013 it was already difficult to get specific visa clearance to allow entry to higher education institutions, with the visa system outsourced to a private company that combines the specific requirements of many different client states and so necessitating a very detailed monitoring of every aspect of an applicant's past. There was a tank parked in the yard opposite the hotel in Moscow, and posters of Putin in the breakfast bar. Near the Starbucks on the Arbat, site of many key scenes in Bulgakov's *Master and Margarita*, a man played the violin in the bitter cold, snow flecks resting on the strings and on his fingers. The GUM department store facing Red Square was full of fancy goods, yet another indication of the rapidly-widening class divide in the capital from which beggars are regularly wiped away, rendered invisible.

If it was cold in Moscow, it was colder in Kazan, about 450 miles east, republic capital of Tatarstan, a city in which that provincial kremlin houses one of the many mosques, this a republic in which just under 40 percent of the population is registered as Muslim. Yeltsin went to kindergarten in Kazan, and Lenin went to university here.

It is possible, though unusual, and cause of great suspicion, to go into Kazan Federal University and find the classroom where Lenin studied law before he was eventually excluded for political activities in 1887. We wandered in blithely asking directions to Lenin's classroom, and worried officials rushed around looking for English-speakers, eventually turning up a friendly librarian who showed us around and who later met up with us to take us into one of the main functioning mosques in the city. That the mosque was situated inside the Kazan Kremlin, it now became clear, was a sign of control and management of Islam by the regime, and of a distinction between good and bad Muslims.

The Lenin House Museum in Kazan was closed for repairs, but workmen let us in to look around. As elsewhere in Russia, there was both stubborn obedient following of the law and numerous loopholes which enabled people to show generosity of spirit in the face of innumerable odds. We were closely watched in the airports and stations, and armed police and military personnel would sidle up to us and stand by waiting in case we did anything unlawful.

We were forbidden by our visas to enter the University in Izhevsk, capital of the Udmurt Republic, a further 175 miles east, but special visitor cards were produced when we arrived in the city which enabled us to get into some of the buildings. The Udmurt Republic was recognised, along with Tatarstan, as a separate entity in 1920 after the revolution, but now there is increasing centralisation and control by Moscow. Things were especially tight because Izhevsk was one of the 'closed cities' in Soviet times; it was the site of industrial weapons production. In 2013, however, it was possible to visit the Kalashnikov factory, view display after display of crooked regime despots around the world holding different versions of the gun, and then go down to the basement and fire one at a target; it's a gun with a violent kickback. Mikhail Kalashnikov was still around in the city, but died two weeks after we left Izhevsk, no connection.

At the Tchaikovsky museum in nearby Votkinsk, from which you could look at the real Swan Lake, we were told that the composer had 'marital problems', but his homosexuality, which was being erased from a Russian biopic of his life, was not mentioned. Discussions of sexuality in Izhevsk were fraught, with official translators choosing the Russian word for 'strange' to explain to a puzzled audience what I was talking about as 'queer'. Putin has clamped down on those who, as the official legal ruling has it, propagate pretend-family relationships; this is something uncannily similar, but more brutal than legislation floated by the Conservatives in Britain in the late 1980s. It is more brutal in Russia because it licenses physical attacks on lesbians and gays.

Engels' classic 1884 text *The Origin of the Family, Private Property and State* had argued that there was an intimate connection between the emergence of class society and the state institutions that defended it and patriarchy, the rule of men over women. This argument was important to the first forging of links between Marxist and feminist politics. Now in modern Russia we had the truth of Engel's thesis displayed; as the capitalist state became more powerful, the nuclear family, already promoted by Stalin while dampening the sexual liberation that accompanied the 1917 revolution, became part of the ideological bedrock of the regime. That meant suppression of homosexuality as a threat to the nuclear family, something that Pussy Riot understood well, and we visited the Cathedral of Christ the Saviour in Moscow where they demonstrated in homage to them. The suicide rate for young women is highest in the world in six of the seven Russian republics.

Discussions about race were sometimes also fraught, with people offering the opinion that London must be dangerous to live in because there are so many black people there. I knew from Ukrainian friends who had visited Moscow recently that to speak their language on the Metro there was dangerous. Our hosts in Izhevsk did not know what to make of the Euromaidan protests in Ukraine that were happening at that time; those who had been brought up as loyal party members, and showed us a statue of Lenin in the city where they had stood guard overnight, asked us of images of Lenin's statue being toppled in Kiev, 'Is this a revolution?' Sexual and national minorities, even if they are not all together 'minorities' at all, are under threat, and ecological activists are also under direct attack. This is clear from the detention of a member of the Trotskyist Russian Socialist Movement in Izhevsk in May 2020 after campaigning against a hazardous waste plant on the edge of the city.

State and Revolution

This is a harsh time to be a revolutionary in Russia, when was it not, and any kind of temptation to ally with the Putin regime on the basis that it is engaged in any kind of progressive struggle against the West should be resisted. This regime is intimately linked to many other brutal regimes around the world, and willing to shift allegiance at a moment's notice depending on its own particular diplomatic interests. This was the case under Stalin who deliberately distorted Lenin's explicit pronouncement that it was not possible to build socialism in one country to make it seem as if the only country that could build socialism would be Russia, and that the state interests of the Soviet Union should be defended above all else. There is a direct line from those days of the bureaucracy that crystallised in the 1920s upon the hard-fought-for 'workers state' to Stalin and then to Putin.

Trotskyists made it a point of principle for many years to defend the political-economic gains of the revolution against the capitalist world even when the bureaucracy was dead-set against the people. With the fall of the Berlin Wall, and the headlong rush to neoliberal capitalism, even that temptation to take sides between Russia and the rest of the capitalist world has fallen away. The irony is that the pull of a kind of 'campist' defence of the Soviet Union that was energetically resisted for many years by some revolutionary Marxists who, from 1948, saw the regime as being 'state capitalist' and so declared a plague on both houses (with the slogan 'neither Washington nor Moscow but International Socialism') have been still powerful now, including on those comrades. There are a multitude of forces pulling Stalinists nostalgic for the old days of the Soviet Union as well as sect-like remains of old state capitalist groups to find something positive in Putin. There is nothing positive in Putin, nor in the macho capitalist nationalist dreams he peddles to the Russian people.

The Soviet regime once served as a template for other progressive movements around the world, and the military might of Stalin and then Krushchev and then Brezhnev enforced that template inside the Communist Parties that were part of the Third International. This model was not only a tragic mistake for revolutionaries of different stripes around the world desperate for support in their own struggles, but also had the effect of blocking solidarity with revolutionaries inside Russia who were trying to redeem the hopes of October, to remain true to the democratic socialist dynamic of the 1917 Revolution. It was a revolution betrayed, and if we are not to repeat those mistakes we need to learn from them, and to do that in solidarity with our comrades around the world wherever they are.

2

GEORGIA

We move south next, four years after the October Revolution, to witness the long-lingering consequences for liberals, social-democrats, Stalinists and revolutionary Marxists of the Menshevik parallel universe that accompanied and resisted Bolshevism in the Caucasus at the crossroads of Eastern Europe and Western Asia.

The October Revolution in Georgia was late-coming, the Russians bringing Soviet rule arrived in 1921. Stalin, born in Georgia, had much to do with the twists and turns of this process, the revolution marked by manipulation and brute force that presaged what was to happen to the October Revolution in Russia itself. The way this overturning of feudal and capitalist rule occurred also introduced severe political-economic distortions into this small republic south of the Caucasus mountain range, a country smaller than the size of Scotland.

Georgia is surrounded, in clockwise panoramic sweep, by Russia to the north, still a prison-house of nations which includes, on the Georgian border, Abkhazia on the Black Sea, North and South Ossetia, Chechnya and Dagestan, then Azerbaijan to the south east, and then, around along the south border, Armenia, Turkey and

Ajara, another controversial, barely acknowledged enclave back on the Black Sea. The Black Sea is west, and the capital Tbilisi is quite far over in the east of the country. The S1 highway from the coast to Tbilisi and beyond has signs to Ankara back west one way and Teheran east to the other, indication, if we needed it, that this place celebrates itself sometimes as the meeting point between Eastern Europe and West Asia, sometimes as the centre of the world.

The end of Soviet times also came late, shadowed again by fraught relations with Russia to the north. Eduard Shevardnadze, First Secretary of the Georgian Communist Party had been appointed by Mikhail Gorbachev as Soviet foreign minister in 1985 to oversee the dismantling of the Cold War, correlate of glasnost and perestroika, and had then appointed himself Head of State in Georgia ten years later, in 1995. The kind of fake 'socialism' that was established in Georgia lasted way after the collapse of the Soviet Union, until the so-called 'Rose Revolution' of 2003.

Five years after that the Russo-Georgian war in 2008 saw bitter defeat, with Russian-occupied Abkhazia, which had already been lost in an earlier bloody border dispute in the 1990s, now joined by South Ossetia, an occupied enclave which can be seen from the S1 highway. Russia moved the border further south a few kilometres recently, significantly closer to Tbilisi, a show of power. That long historical arc of imposed 'revolution' and then late 'counterrevolution' which brought liberal democratic multiparty rule gives to Georgia a particular cultural-political complexion, and particular contradictions which continue to erupt in protests that have an uncanny 'red-brown' character that continues what is now a mostly covert relationship with Russia under Putin.

Before Stalinism

Josef Vissarionovich Djugahsvili was born in Gori in the centre of Georgia, in the Russian quarter of the town, in 1878 or 1879, depending on who you believe and when it was convenient for celebrations to mark significant birthdays after he assumed complete power at the head of the Soviet bureaucracy. Djugashvili, later Stalin, studied, with a scholarship, to be a priest in the Georgian Apostolic Autocephalous Orthodox Church – Orthodox Christianity was then the state religion – at a seminary in Tbilisi, enrolling in 1894 and expelled five years later. He then worked for a couple of years as an accountant, record-keeper, bureaucrat at the Tbilisi Meteorological and Geophysical Observatory before going underground. It was then, from 1901 onwards in the Caucasus and Russia, with spells in prison in Siberia, that he honed his skills as organiser, staging bank robberies and mobilising workers on strike in Batumi on the Black Sea coast and in Baku, capital of Azerbaijan. The Stalin Museum in Gori is one of the few places in Georgia where you will find outright celebration of the man.

Georgians with the franchise for state power in Tbilisi from 1921 through to 2003 were always in close contact with their compatriots in Moscow, whether that was Stalin himself at the beginning or Shevardnadze at the end, and the massive Italianate Museum in Gori was built in 1957 next to Josef Djugashivili's birthplace – a little house protected by a mausoleum-style structure round the corner from the Stalin train which ferried him safely around his realm. This construction was undertaken a year after Krushchev's speech denouncing his former paymaster. The Museum was officially closed in 1989, year of the fall of the Berlin Wall and effectively the collapse of the Soviet Union, but slowly opened again on Stalin Avenue without fanfare, and so that's where the tatty memorabilia of Soviet Georgian times is to be found. Elsewhere in Georgia, questions about Stalin get evasive answers or a frosty reception. You won't find much post-socialist nostalgia in Georgia, and neither has Trotskyism taken root there for various reasons rooted in the early history of the old regime.

This question of Stalin and the Soviet period in Georgia is resolutely avoided and bypassed in bizarre tourist-targeted appeals to a past golden age of Georgian culture when, if we are to believe it, this was Colchis, site of the Golden Fleece, quest of Jason and the Argonauts, with Golden Fleece festivals appearing in the early 21st century to mark this particular 'invention of tradition'. Georgian wine is relentlessly marketed as being fruit of the oldest wine in the world, evidence dredged up of wines dating back 6,000 years, and this alongside special double-editions of BBC Radio 4's 'Food Programme' celebrating the wine and, we were told there, vegetarian food which is all the more widespread because there are so many Orthodox Church festivals during which meat and fish is prohibited. The Shotis Puri bread is still fresh-baked on the interior wall of kilns in local bakeries, as is the honey-bread around Surami on the S1 highway. The home-made wines are cooked up in huge earthenware underground 'qvevris'; this cottage industry production, together with some of the larger chichi wine estates, now replaces the much-resented and much muttered about 'standardisation' of wine under the Soviets.

There are many different communities, including Christians, of course, and Muslims, especially in the south closer to the borders with Azerbaijan and Turkey. There are also local long-standing Kurdish communities, mainly Yazidi. In Batumi on the border with Turkey, now a tourist playground for Arab-state visitors as well as Russians venturing south from Abkhazia just up the coast, there is an Ali and Nino 'Statue of Love' to commemorate the fictional characters in the popular novel by Kurban Said, a Romeo and Juliet-style romance between Ali the Azerbaijani Muslim and Princess Nino his Georgian Christian lover.

The story of Ali and Nino is supposed to speak of toleration, but actually, first published in Vienna in 1937, speaks more of the poisoning of personal relationships as a function of imperial great-power conflict. Despite the oft-repeated claims that this was one of the few places in Europe to welcome different competing Jewish communities – and there are still two rival synagogues close by each other in Tbilisi – the famous 'mountain Jew' communities no longer exist, and the wooden synagogue in Kulashi was empty, as was the nearby Jewish Museum set up by an ex-policeman and, it turned out when the caretaker came to open it up, was mainly devoted to links with Israel.

This area around Kutaisi, now the main decaying post-industrial base for the region, had been the site both of the Guria peasant rebellion in 1904, one in which something like a commune had been set up, and site of some of the key protests leading up the Rose Revolution nearly a century later. The caretaker for the Kulashi synagogue who showed us around wore a large wooden crucifix. Stepping back past the legacy of Stalin and Stalinism also enables the question of Stalin's own antisemitism to be politely overlooked. A 'New Communist Party' was founded in 2001 by Yevgeny Dzhugashvili, the grandson of Joseph Stalin, and stood in parliamentary elections, but only in Ajara in the south-west of the country, a provocation linked to Russian attempts to stoke a local secessionist movement in the area around Batumi on the Turkish border, a secessionist movement designed to put further pressure on the Tbilisi regime.

Stalin, unfortunately, is intimately linked with the history of the 'socialist' years of the regime, and in a much deeper way than in Russia, where there were at least a few years of freedom, of experimentation with new ways of living that the October Revolution opened up. In Georgia, another route to 'socialism', that of the social-democratic Second International was opened up by the bourgeois-democratic 'February' revolution in 1917, but then shut down again.

There had been Marxist groups in Georgia going back to 1892 with the formation of 'The Third Group', and there were peasant rebellions (with the Guria uprising ranking at one time as high as that of the Paris Commune among

Russian Marxists as an inspiration) but revolutionary organisation became closely tied to the internal debates and splits in the Russian Social Democratic Labour Party (RSDLP). That party, the RSDLP, split at its second congress, in London in 1903, into the Bolsheviks and the Mensheviks. Then this split, despite or because of Stalin's activities in the Caucasus, resulted in the formation of a strong Menshevik party, the Georgia Social Democratic Party, and a smaller but more militant communist party, the Bolsheviks.

The Russian February 1917 formation of a Provisional Government is marked in Stalinist historiography as a 'bourgeois democratic' revolution because it accords well with a quasi-Marxist 'stage' theory of history in which there must first be a bourgeois-democratic stage – which in Russia would be the unfeasibly quick implantation of capitalism – before the socialist stage in October later that year. The Bolsheviks seized power in Russia, but in Georgia elections for a Constituent Assembly designed to lay the foundations for a bourgeois-democratic republic went ahead, and the local Menshevik 'Georgia Social Democratic Party' won by a large majority.

The new regime rapidly made diplomatic and trade links with the German occupying forces and then with the British who replaced the Germans at the end of the First World War in 1918. The German and then British forces were keen to work with the Menshevik government as one that would guarantee the protection of large private property, foreign investment and, crucially, support for General Denikin's Volunteer Army, one of the invasion forces worsening the Civil War inside the new Soviet

Union. (Denikin died in Ann Arbor, Michigan, in 1947.) The Bolsheviks in Georgia understandably needed to defeat Denikin and bring the Russian October Revolution south in order to protect it, and launched several coup attempts against the Menshevik regime before the Red Army finally entered the country in 1921. It is this period between 1917 and 1921 that is vaunted by contemporary supporters of the Second International as the lost time of Georgian democratic socialism, most notably in Eric Lee's 2017 *The Experiment: Georgia's Forgotten Revolution 1918-1921.*

What is undoubtedly the case, and with grave consequences for the formation of the new Soviet republic in Georgia, was that Stalin was already mobilising his supporters in Moscow to prevent Lenin and Trotsky from realising what was going on, and inside Georgia to install a regime that would, avant la lettre, be Stalinist. The invasion force was led by one of Stalin's loyal compatriots Sergo Ordzhonikidze, already a bad sign, and despite Lenin's explicit orders that the Red Army should act with respect to the Georgians and try and win their support, Stalin pressed ahead in his usual style. The head of the Cheka, Lavrentiy Beria, was moved from Baku to Georgia in 1920, and then appointed by Stalin to oversee counter-insurgency strategy, setting up the local secret police.

The Red Army invasion of Georgia led prominent Second International social democrats, such as Karl Kautsky, to leap to the defence of the supposedly 'democratic socialist' regime and launch a tirade against Bolshevism in 1921 in *Georgia: A Social-Democratic Peasant Republic – Impressions and Observations* after his visit to the country. This led Trotsky, as head of the Red Army, and one-time Menshevik himself, to respond to Kautsky in 1922 in *Between Red and White: A Study of Some Fundamental Questions of Revolution, With Particular Relevance to Georgia.* That reply to Kautsky had the unfortunate and unexpected effect of implicating Trotsky in Stalin's manoeuvres back in Russia in the eyes of a good number of Georgian Marxists.

The legacy of the Soviet era is visible in the bureacratised processes through which you must pass if you are off the usual tourist routes. For example, in the town of Gurjaani in the far-east of the country, there is a health resort with mud baths, the sulphurous wet earth bubbling up from the ground in a public park. The Soviet-style concrete cultural centre in the centre of town is an empty wreck. We have been in mud baths in north Greece near the border with Bulgaria – an informal stroll through the showers and down into the immense thick brown puddles with frogs lounging around the edge – but this was entirely different, entirely medicalised. No one spoke English, and we spoke neither Georgian nor Russian; and so, through a complex convoluted sign exchange, we mimed that we wanted to visit the mud baths and were directed to the administrative buildings where our passports were demanded of us so we could register for our visit to the 'clinic'.

The options at Resort Akhtala included an apartment for one day at 10 GEL, a good deal, or 'Electric Mud' also at 10 GEL or, a little more expensive, a 'Rectal Swab' at 12 GEL. We just wanted the plain mud experience. It was there that the typical Soviet system of obstacles and loopholes came into play; we did not have passports with us but, they indicated with a knowing look, we could perhaps 'remember' the numbers, and then, after we had registered, we went to the clinic where our blood pressure was taken – no other medical history was possible in the absence of a shared language – and we were ushered into the waiting corridor. Men and women were taken separately and put in large warm porcelain mud-filled baths where they lay for 20 minutes before they were taken out to have their showers. We lay in the baths, four baths arranged in the room, and watched the clock.

The metro system in Tbilisi is typical post-Soviet design with very little advertising, a grim if tidy journey from the centre out to the working-class estates where friendly drunks roam the streets helpfully misdirecting you to your small bed and breakfast which looks, in the booking dot com picture as if it is a palace when it is actually tucked behind a small unpainted wooden gate at the end of a cul de sac. In our case, the gate sign was painted during the day after we arrived; we had appeared, to the extreme surprise of the owner, as his first ever guests. We were distracted by the men with qvevri-wine while the women stripped the room of its inhabitants and bedding and prepared it for us. On our last evening we were invited to dinner and watched the family dance to music videos on their lap-top in which old Georgian melodies were matched, on the screen, with images of partisans fighting in the first war against the Russians in Abkhazia in 1992. Many booking dot com photos of places in the countryside depict gangs of men in wife-beater vests standing by beat-up cars glaring at the camera. Refurbished cars are a main export product, and many cars have bits missing, matching the state of the roads, including the pot-holed Tbilisi bypass in spitting distance of the South Ossetia border.

The legacy of the Soviet era is also very much present in ongoing hostility to Russians, of which there are still many in the shape not only as occupiers of twenty percent of Georgian territory in the north of the country (with threats by Putin to lop off another portion, Ajara in the south-west), but also as tourists. If you don't speak Georgian you will be asked if you speak Russian, and when you say you do not, there will often be a palpable sense of relief and, probably as a counter-reaction, extreme friendliness.

The spa town of Borjomi, now in a national park, has been a favourite watering-hole for Russian visitors since the mid-nineteenth century. There are 150 thermal springs in the area, rediscovered by the Russian army returning home from fighting Turks and developed as a summer residence by the viceroy of the Transcaucasus Grand Duke Mikhail Nikolayevich Romanov, brother of the Tsar between 1862 and 1871, an ambitious colonial project. Smudged photos of Tsars and Tsarinas and various other notables, including Chekhov and Tchaikovsky, adorn the run-down villa adjoining the central spa area which ejects sulphurous water, and through the gates of Ekaterina Park you can trek a couple of miles to bathe in the waters at an open-air pool, also now still full of Russians. The men laughed, and none of the women tending the kids even smiled. Just north of Batumi on the coast we shared a balcony that stretched the length of our accommodation with three jolly Russian women who laughed a lot, until four in the morning, during which time they drank and sang, and replayed recordings of their singing on their mobile phones.

From Red to Rose Revolutions

The collapse of the Soviet Union and then success of the Georgian Rose Revolution, have opened up at least two competing cultural-political tendencies, both of which are riddled with their own contradictions. The first, following from the privatisation of state resources and the capitalisation of cultural assets, is an intensification of neoliberalism. There are offices and scam companies aplenty in Tbilisi adorned with NATO and EU paraphernalia, a promise that the locals can get a piece of the economic action by really being part of the West. One of my new Facebook friends who ran a bed and breakfast in Georgia now sends me messages inviting me to invest in this or that new firm, 'American', he says, a firm that is guaranteed to give a good profit return.

Tourists, from Russia, Turkey, Israel (to name those we met and compared notes with) as well as from Western Europe, will pay at some point to drink qvevri wine and eat cheese and walnuts and maybe more depending on how much they are willing to spend at a staged 'supra'. This sometimes elaborate meal, the supra, which should include speeches by the host and guests, is packaged and sold as an authentic Georgian folk experience, though it is possible, on occasion, to stumble across a small house with an image of a qvevri on a board hanging outside the gate and have some real fun. At one wine-cellar we were given wine, cheese and walnuts in set pomegranate paste, a speciality that you see hanging from stalls at the side of the S1 highway, but we had to hurry because a coach party of Latvians had already booked in for their own pre-booked supra experience.

Our worst supra was on the edge of Sighnaghi, a fortress town near the border with Azerbaijan, where the meal ritual was overseen by a US-American guy called Paul. He was a retired businessman in a funny black hat (kind of ethnic, but the type of which we saw no one else around wear) who had managed to discover some tendentious connection with his Georgian heritage after the Rose Revolution and had moved out east to make a killing in the concrete-construction business while running supras for the tourists as his hobby. Paul was practised in coercive control, and tapped you on the head with his pointy stick if you drank your wine before you heard his spiel and then gave your own little speech. Here was neoliberalism in action; iron-laws of the market protected by the state for new colonial enterprises to buy up local industries and sell them on. Not everyone was out to fleece you, however, and we were given Shotis Puri bread for free in villages when we peered into the bakery; an old guy in the ethnographic museum in Sighnaghi wanted money, but not Euros because he already had some of those, he was just collecting the notes.

Here was clear evidence, in reverse, that Trotsky was right when he formulated the law of combined and uneven development that underpins his 1905 theory of 'permanent revolution'. There is no fixed unfolding sequence to the stages of history – as if there must be primitive communism characterised by scarcity and misery, then the rise of class society, with slavery and then feudalism and then capitalism, and only after that socialism and a return to full communism characterised by technological success and abundance – but a potentially uninterrupted process by which one form of struggle can 'grow over' into the next. It is potentially uninterrupted, but it is often blocked, as it is when the Stalinised Communist Parties that hold the 'stage' conception of history to be true ensure that it is; they then also thereby prevent bourgeois-democratic independence movements fulfilling their task in the only way they ever could, by nationalising the means of production and effectively turning into socialists, something that Castro discovered in Cuba.

The 'stage' conception was ruthlessly implemented as a distortion of Marxist politics by Stalin, but before that, here in this part of the world, the Menshevik Georgia Social Democratic Party tried to put the brakes on historical development. One of the paradoxes of supposedly 'anti-Stalinist' Second International praise for the Georgia 'experiment' is that advocates of this Menshevik approach themselves also tell us quite clearly that a leap into the task of socialist revolution would have been too fast, too soon. Not for nothing was Georgia one of the sites of debate about the so-called 'Asiatic mode of development' as a way-station and exception to Marx's own discussions of the transition from feudalism to capitalism in different parts of the world. Now, as a social-democratic political orientation that keeps itself carefully inside the limits set by bourgeois-democratic neoliberal capitalist society in Georgia, we see historical stages of 'development' run as if backwards. Trotsky's theory of permanent revolution escaped from that rigid grid, and also helps us make sense now of how quickly this supposedly 'socialist' society could transform itself into a neoliberal one.

The second cultural-political tendency at work in Georgia now is, in some ways, worse. Here there is a most peculiar alliance between the far-right – a political force intent on wiping out both the legacy of socialism and the liberal reforms that ease the transition to neoliberalism – and the Orthodox Church. This is not to say that every Christian believer in Georgia is allied with the far right, but this is an intensely religious country in which the tolerant and mystical tradition also succours some more dangerous fundamentalist movements. This is not to pretend that religion was simply 'repressed' when Georgia was a Soviet Republic, and that it then erupted again when the lid was taken off, any more than to it is to say that ancient wine varieties waiting to flourish found a way to do so after the mean times, bursting free. In both cases we need a clearer, more elaborate, historical-materialist account of the way that countervailing political-economic forces at any particular moment are constructed.

At a supra in Kakheti, a schoolteacher told us, with the aid of a neighbour who spoke some English, that we must visit Mtskheta to the north-west of Tbilisi because, she said, Jesus Christ himself had visited it when he was in Georgia. Our translator, who was a retired academic from the department of sociology in the University of Tbilisi, wasn't so sure this was true. In the wooded countryside outside the village of Akhasheni just north of Gurjaani, we sought out one of the Orthodox monasteries. People were mystified when we made the sign of a cross and pointed into the distance, and they indicated that the place we were aiming for was much too far away. Eventually a man we asked took pity on us, turfed his family out of his car, and drove us five miles or more alongside the bare drought-hit river into the trees, and then into a glade where a little cluster of houses stood around an old church. He dropped us and waved goodbye, and, while we were worrying about how we would get back, we ventured into the church.

An Orthodox priest with a big beard and black hat came to meet us, and, grinning the while, gave us a tour, and showed us beautiful gold-edged but unfinished paintings of saints in the small dining room. There were, he said – I said 'said', but this was in sign language – three of them, three priests living there, the others were out that afternoon. He made us some instant coffee, offered us sweets, and then gave us sweet wine, and finally, thank the lord, made the sign of driving a car, after which he drove us back to the main road. There are also religious fundamentalists in the cities who are mobilising their flock to protest against the liberalisation of drug laws – possession and consumption of cannabis was legalised in Georgia in 2018 though it is still illegal to cultivate or sell it – and these are the kind of guys who are behind some of the most reactionary and vicious Georgian political mobilisations now going on.

Three years before our 2018 visit far-right activists wearing rings of sausages around their necks and wielding skewers stacked with slabs of meat attacked the 'Kiwi' vegan café in a quiet side-street of the capital Tbilisi. 'Georgia for the Georgians', a favourite slogan for a range of religious nationalist groups and hard-core Nazis, had been a rallying cry for demonstrations in Tbilisi over the previous weeks. Fascist meat-eaters would not like this café, true; one large poster on the wall read 'Seahorses against Gender Roles'. Up the hill nearby there was a sticker on a lamppost that read 'FCK NZS'. Over the last couple of years vegetarianism has been on the nationalist radar along with gay rights, both seen as 'Western' imports.

'Vegetarian' and 'gay' function in these reactionary protests as alarming signifiers of all that is bad and foreign in a small country that has historically defined itself as being at the crossroads of the West and Asia. Most recent protests have been against Russians, joyfully reported by Radio Free Europe, the peculiar paradox here being that while such rhetoric is very easily activated among a population with understandable antipathy to Russia, there is good evidence that Putin has been funding some of the far-right groups involved (as he has been in funding Jobbik in Hungary and Le Pen in France).

So-called 'tradition' in Georgia, as in other places is, in reality, what Eric Hobsbawm and Terence Ranger dubbed in the title of their 1983 edited book an *'Invention of Tradition'*. Authentic buried national forces do not lie buried beneath the surface in the way mystical anti-Marxist writers ranging from Madame Blavatsky (who visited the Borjomi spa town in her time) to George Gurdjieff (who settled, with his followers, briefly in Tbilisi in 1919 before relocating to Batumi) would claim. Marxist accounts of the 'invention of tradition' are designed to show us how what appears to be so deep within a culture is actually constructed and reconstructed according to present-day needs. Neither is there a naturally-unfolding irreversible process of change running through identifiable stages of political-economic development over the course of history. Instead, as Trotsky argued, there are strange leaps, and now we know that there are also strange reversals of fortune, of progressive movements and of societies that seemed once to have been able to break from capitalism and build something better now seeming to regress, leap backwards. Those leaps and reversals are also always structured – they do not happen in a mystical way independent of human collective agency – and our task is to understand how they are organised s we can organise our own lives differently.

The invention of tradition together with our understanding of what 'revolution' is in Georgia is riddled with paradoxes. The uncertain ambiguous character of the country is at stake in the new definitions of politics and identity raging there now in the wake of what was once mistakenly called 'socialism', but which was always in different strange ways but a caricature of what we hope for in the world.

3

REPUBLIC OF SERBIA

Next stab at socialism comes in Eastern Europe at the end of the Second World War, in a country heavily indebted to the Soviet Union but then able to defy Stalin and so open up hopes for a revolutionary Marxist renaissance so that what we thought of as a template for a socialist society is remade, found again but then lost.

Serbia, with just over seven million people, is isolated. Once the centre of the Socialist Federal Republic of Yugoslavia, SFRY, it was led by Josip Broz Tito as head of the League of Communists of Yugoslavia from 1945 after successful partisan struggle during the war until Tito's death in 1980. Serbia has been dismembered during a bloody civil war in the 1990s. It is now land-locked, edged to the east and north by former Soviet bloc countries which it dramatically broke from in 1948 – Bulgaria, Romania and Hungary – and to the north-west, west and south by its former associated republics in the federation, Croatia, Montenegro, Kosovo and Macedonia. Even the naming of these other rival entities in this context is now filled with dispute and unresolved enmity. Serbia stands alone, with the exception – an irony of history – of Russia. The country is now increasing trade-links with China.

The break with Stalin in 1948 opened up a period of so-called 'self-management socialism' and some degree of freedom of manoeuvre for leftist dissidents and intellectuals who were then able to connect with the anti-Stalinist left outside the country. Meetings that included the 'Praxis' philosophers functioned as a relay-point for radical ideas not only from Marxist traditions outside Yugoslavia, including from the Fourth International, but also for a current of Yugoslav thought that was re-thinking what was possible in conditions of isolation. Tito tried to break that isolation of Yugoslavia through active participation in the Non-Aligned Movement (NAM) which was founded in 1956 at Brioni (which is now in Croatia), a movement which now continues with 120 nation-state members.

The Yugoslav experiment thus became a touchstone for many socialists looking for an alternative to the Soviet model, an alternative to Stalinism, but it failed, and the reasons it failed ripple on through Serbia today. It was a country that attempted to build socialism in one republic under siege, under pressure both from Stalinist Eastern Europe faithful to Moscow and from capitalist Western Europe determined to undermine any claim for the success of an anti-capitalist alternative. This process must, as Catherine Samary argues, be understood in the context of the attempt at and then defeat of 'decolonial communism'.

That experiment failed not only because it was isolated but also because 'self-management socialism' was a fiction that patched together workers in different competing local enterprises with a state in which there was still the iron-grip of the League of Communists, an apparatus of censorship that held the regime in place.

Eat cake

Now with the destruction of the old socialism what remains is authoritarian nostalgia and intolerance of difference. On 10 May 2017, shortly before our visit, Bernard-Henri Lévi, one of the leading figures in the right-wing Nouveaux Philosophes group in France in the 1970s, got a cake in his face at the Belgrade Cultural Center. The protest against Lévi was orchestrated by Novi SKOJ, a 'communist' youth group with a tiny membership but control of one of the old League of Communists headquarters. The Novi SKOJ activists unfurled a banner (in English) reading 'Bernard Levy advocates imperialist murders' and they shouted abuse at Lévi over his support for the 1999 NATO bombing of Serbia. The SKOJ website declares itself to be against imperialist intervention in Cuba and Venezuela, and a young activist interviewed on the radio after the event declared that China was a good model for economic commonsense combined with socialist values.

The cake protest is indicative of the level of continued anger in Serbia, not only at the bombing as such, but of the isolation of the regime, with some politicians keen to take Serbia into the European Community, and others closer to Putin. The anger flows into disruption of cultural events that appear to be in line with Western European agendas, into seething resentment at the dismantling of the old socialist state structures, and into nationalist protest that spills quickly over into racism, including antisemitism. It is no accident, perhaps, that Lévi (in Belgrade to launch his 2016 film *Peshmerga*) was attacked; a prominent Jewish intellectual, he fits the bill as one of the visible enemies onto which the woes of the old Stalinist forces, now willing to engage in red-brown alliances to match what is happening in Russia and Georgia and elsewhere in the old Soviet bloc can project their hatred. One young activist told me again about the incident but said the protest was against the French anthropologist Claude Lévi-Strauss, an innocent slip we laughed about at the time but could have explored further; such ideological motifs we all relay as we speak, almost oblivious of their manifold contradictory meanings.

There was sympathy in Belgrade in 2017, even among some ostensible leftists, with the Viktor Orbán regime in Hungary that is busy demonising George Soros as the architect of Western intellectual intervention. As the Slovene Slavoj Žižek has pointed out, one of the signifiers of antisemitic discourse in the Balkans today is 'Soros', emblematic of the current paranoid fascination with the idea that Jews are deliberately arranging the migration of the Muslim hordes from the Arab world into Europe, with Serbia one of the first stops for this Judaic-Islamic destruction of their own culture. Remember that Žižek himself had declared during the NATO bombing that it was 'too little, too late', a phrase that was quickly removed from later versions of his widely circulated discussion of the events at the time, and his face appears graffitied on Belgrade buildings with the cryptic legend (in Serbian Roman script) 'Sing like Slavoj' (a pun on his name, which is similar in sound to that of a small songbird in Serbian).

While SKOJ represents one of the most regressive and marginal nationalist strands of 'Yugostalgia' – a local variant of nostalgia for the old socialism – there are other variants of this kind of politics at the centres of power. The party of Slobodan Milošević – the Socialist Party of Serbia (with only a Cyrillic website) – is in coalition with the Democratic Party and with the newly-elected nationalist president Aleksandar Vučić, who is currently head of the Progressive Party (Srpska Napredna Stranka – SNS) but well-known as a one-time activist with the far-right 'Radical Party'. Vučić served as minister of information under Milošević. Protests reached 50,000 on the streets after Vučić's election in April 2017. The April Belgrade street protests were partly about voting irregularities, but also about the austerity, privatisation and 'security' measures reinforced by the Vučić regime. The SNS and the Socialist Party effectively co-opt 'socialist' rhetoric about the good old days while steering the country in a neoliberal direction. There is also a tiny Communist Party of Serbia run by its President Joška Broz, Tito's grandson. The Serbian Government website judiciously balances support for various dictatorships that will engage in economic deals.

Once strongly opposed to the EU, Vučić is pushing negotiations to join it. And he is rewarded by kind words from Angela Merkel who is more than happy to overlook Vučić's youthful flirtation with fascism and current authoritarian policies; while Merkel presents herself to her

European audience as tolerant generous host to refugees, a strong state in Serbia is perfect for her insofar as it functions as a heavily securitised state apparatus to prevent refugees from the Arab world crossing its borders and so then making their way to Germany. Anti-immigrant practice is in this way encouraged inside Serbia. In early May 2017 the Serbian Commissariat for Refugees and Immigration forcibly removed 1,200 refugees from the centre of Belgrade on the pretext that the building needed to be demolished. The officials carrying out the evacuation wore protective clothing and sprayed the refugees from Afghanistan and the Arab world with disinfectant. There were protests by NGOs working with asylum-seekers, and there is some grassroots mobilisation by progressive groups like 'No Border Serbia'.

There is a deep antisemitic and nationalist dynamic in much mainstream organised politics which is fuelled by a particular preoccupation with Serb identity under threat and with the centrifugal process that was unleashed in the final years of the Socialist Federal Republic. There is, for example, a motif of victim-hood that Milošević used in order to mobilise the Serbs as the chosen people, even in some representations of them as being the equivalent of the Jews suffering at the hands of external agents; this simultaneously with a dose of covert antisemitism in which the implication was that those external agents were conspiring to destroy the Serb nation, agents such as Soros (sometimes with Soros as ringleader). Not incidentally, many of the anecdotes that spatter Žižek's writing are from a popular big book of Jewish jokes published in Belgrade in the 1970s.

The defining moment of Milošević's turn from anything approaching socialism to full-blown nationalism came after his visit to Kosovo in 1989 and his declaration in his Gazimistan speech that the Serbs must redeem their defeat at the Battle of Kosovo in 1389. This defining moment 600 years in the past functioned, according to some analysts, as the 'chosen trauma' of the Serbs under Milošević, and it positioned them as victims with a mission to overturn the oppression to which they had been subjected. It is a victim motif that recurs in Serbia today whenever the question of self-determination of Kosovo is mentioned; the spectre is raised that the Kosovans really want to take a third of Serbian territory, that there must be limits to self-determination because the Kosovans will not limit themselves to their own territory (and, alongside that argument, there is often the claim that the Kosovan territory is itself actually always already Serb). This is the soil into which are planted ridiculous stereotypes about the 'Serbian mentality' that some of the nationalist locals wallow in, rehearsed in many books for sale in the many bookshops.

As Goran Musić points out in his 2013 study (published in Serbian and English by the Rosa Luxemburg Stiftung) *Serbia's Working Class in Transition 1988-2013*, there was a deadly oscillation between two different ideological strategies employed by Milošević. On the one hand, the regime, even before its disintegration in the 1980s, based its rule on workplace units, the 'Basic Organisations of Associated Labour', and this economic decentralisation effectively incited competition between different enterprises (and between industrially stronger and weaker parts of the republic that eventually became configured around specific local nationalist agendas). The nomenclature positioned itself, Musić argues, as a kind of 'social glue', and in this way the regime was able to define the class interests of the Yugoslav working class as national interests. At one moment there was a call for pro-market initiatives which set different groups of workers against each other, and at the next there were attempts to define what counted as 'working class' in order to represent society as a whole.

This oscillation and contradiction between competitive local enterprise as the basis of working-class identity and a general overarching definition of shared national identity – the shared overall project of self-management socialism – came to a head in the 1980s when the economic crisis was addressed primarily through pro-market initiatives that explicitly set the different republics against each other. This led Serbia to define itself not only as the central guiding state apparatus but also against Croatia, Macedonia and Slovenia (which was being levered out of Yugoslavia by way of German capital investment). Musić argues that this process then led to the Serbian nation emerging as the key ideological motif and strategic centre-piece for guaranteeing the power of the bureaucracy under Milošević: 'By placing it in the role of victim of imperialism and bureaucratic machinations, the Serbian nation as a whole was assigned with attributes once reserved for the proletariat. In official language, the term "working class" was starting to be used interchangeably with the term "Serbian people", only to be completely overtaken by it a few years later on'.

This is, indeed, one of the fruits of 'socialism in one country' into which is stirred the poison of victimhood and corresponding search for malevolent external forces, puppet-masters who might be blamed for Serbia's predicament. Musić describes the spate of factory protests and even occupations that were tangled up with the privatisation process through which members of the apparatus were able to transfer ownership into their own hands. The protests were thus also tangled up with that process, unable to defeat it.

White City

Serbia's capital Belgrade, with less than two million people, means 'White City', a name unfortunately relevant during the contemporary refugee crisis and the response of the authorities to immigrants, including Kosovans. There is a small Roma and Chinese community in the city. The Belgrade Fortress at the confluence of the Danube and Sava functions as a national park laid out, the signs say, 'in the English style'. The fortress was an Ottoman stronghold – there are the remains of a hamam in the grounds – and the fortress then functioned as a site of resistance to the Turks and other enemies of the Serbs. The fortress area includes a military museum and, in one of the sunken moat fortifications next to the dinosaur park (filled with not-quite life-like animatronics) there are displays of tanks and NATO equipment seized in 1999. There is a meteorite museum which rehearses one of the commonplace plaints, with a placard inside saying 'Unfortunately, because of everything that happened in our country over the past 100 years, the fate of these meteorites remains unknown'.

On the plinth of a monument in the Fortress Park erected in 1930 in gratitude to the French for its help to Serbia during World War One was a rain-sodden poster with images of some of those murdered in the 78 days of bombing (with the names in Cyrillic) and the legend 'NATO We will never forgive you for killing our children' (in English). The main pedestrianised shopping street, Knez Mihailova, is lined with Western store-names and fetches onto the nearby informal market-stalls in the grounds of the fortress which sell old Tito-era military uniform hats and party-badges, mugs with Tito's face printed on, T-shirts with Putin on, and, next to those, some more emblazoned with images of the celebrated war criminals Radovan Karadžić and Ratko Mladić.

The small town of Zemun, where now-president Vučić went to high school, is on the Danube about an hour walk from Novi Beograd, and is base of the B92 radio station, a Greek-owned outfit that was one of the sources of alternative news during the 1999 NATO bombing but which today pumps out a weird post-truth mixture of US-American programmes and pro-Putin propaganda from Sputnik. Novi Beograd, a housing and shopping complex on one side of the Sava facing the old main city of Belgrade on the other bank, also includes the Soviet-style architect-nightmare block for what was once the Federal Executive Council of Yugoslavia (still used for public functions as the 'Palace of Serbia' to impress foreign dignitaries) and the League of Communists tower block that was badly hit during the bombing, and which is only a few hundred metres from housing blocks (some of the occupants of which were injured during that time).

Language is one of the battlegrounds, with increasing use of English in the media, and Cyrillic is one of the markers of that battleground, indicating adherence to a distinctive 'Serbian' identity that has been manufactured since the split with Croatia and with the other Yugoslav republics. Once 'Serbo-Croat', now the digraphic language of Serbia (that is, written in two different scripts with the same meaning) is torn between the Roman script which is used in Croatia and the other ex-republics, and Cyrillic which also serves to tie Serbia closer to Russia. The political battle over Cyrillic and Roman script is over-determined by class. For example, some digraphic street-names in central Belgrade have been defaced, with stickers or graffiti obscuring the Roman version of the names. And, at the same time, the Saturday night performance of *Aida* in the National Theatre – a glittering golden palace of culture which packed nearly seventy performers onto the stage on one point – was surtitled in Cyrillic script. The mainstream broadsheet press is still published in Cyrillic (as is official documentation in the university), while the tabloid press, which includes one simply called *'Tabloid'*, is in Roman script.

There is elaborate graffiti around the waterfront, along the Danube and the Sava which flows down from Slovenia, once the northernmost republic in the Socialist Federal Republic of Yugoslavia, including the SKOJ tagline 'Yankees go home' (in English) and 'Crimea is

Russian' (in Cyrillic). Most graffiti, apart from the pro-Putin stuff and some 'freedom of movement' slogans (in English), is non-political, including a number of brightly-coloured images with the tag-line 'Go Vegan' (most in English but some in Cyrillic transliterated from the English rather than in actual Serbian), and one of the best vegetarian restaurants – Radost House – has no public signage. Visitors wander up and down the road peering in the windows before the waiter comes out and says 'I guess you are looking for me'. The restaurant-owner is apparently against a sign for his restaurant, I was told, for 'political reasons'.

The interval announcement during the performance of *Aida* at the National Theatre included advertising for a private health company, to the fury of some in the audience but with bland acceptance by most. Public education and healthcare are in the firing line along with housing. Now the privatisation process is being intensified, and that is another reason Merkel loves Vučić, and most of that privatisation is tied to foreign investment in Serbia, a process which also intensifies nationalist resentment and a nationalist spin on protest specifically against 'finance capital' (another code-phrase that can, in this context, be freighted with antisemitism).

In another 2016 document produced by the Rosa Luxemburg Stiftung, Ivan Radenković's *Foreign Direct Investments in Serbia*, Aleksandar Vučić is quoted as saying that Serbia's workforce is lazy, inefficient and accustomed to working under the rules of socialist self-management, something he also refers to as 'mob' mentality. Against this, Vučić argues, Serbia needs a German work ethic, and foreign investment will enable this, not only through the injection of capital but also through the work discipline that will be imposed in the process. Radenković points out that, contrary to the public claims by the government, wages in foreign-owned factories in Serbia range from the minimum wage – that is bare minimum – and barely 20 percent more than that.

Again, the problems stem not only from the recent neoliberal turn under a far-right president, but have their roots in economic 'reforms' undertaken under Tito. Economic reforms from 1965 onwardpromoted integration into international markets, and amendments to the Law on the Funds of Economic Organisations in 1967 created a legal basis for importing capital in the form of joint venture investments. New laws in 1978 and 1988 enabled all kinds of foreign investments. The largest foreign investments in Serbia are now Telenor (Norwegian), Gazprom Neft (Russian), Fiat (Italian), Delhaize (Belgian) and Philip Morris (US-American).

There was very little authentic socialist presence in the 2017 elections. One of the most successful fringe candidates was a comedian running for the 'You haven't tried the stuffed cabbage' party. He came third with nearly ten percent of the vote. There is also a monarchist movement. In 2008 students at the University of Belgrade founded a group called King's Youth which has now established itself as the Kingdom of Serbia Association dedicated to restoring Prince Aleksandar to the throne in a 'constitutional monarchy'. The Prince returned to Serbia in 2001 and lives with his wife in one of the former palaces. 123,000 signatures had been gathered by May 2017 toward the target 150,000 which, the Association claims, will enable them, without a referendum, to restore the Karadjordjevic dynastic line that ruled Serbia until 1945 when the Yugoslav Republic was declared.

Left Summits

There is, however, also a flourishing of alternative movements and the April protests against Vučić indicate that socialism of some kind, after what one young activist described to me as the 'dead blank years of the 1990s', is being reborn. This includes a small Trotskyist presence, a political current demonised by the various Yugostalgic Stalinist groups. I attended a Monday evening meeting at the OCTOBAR radical space in Belgrade that brought together members of different radical social movements. The space is entered through a nondescript doorway off a side-street, down some badly-lit tiled steps and through a plate-steel door with a second intercom entry system. There was a fascist attack on the centre last year. Inside there is a bar, an open patio area and meeting rooms, and, a humanising presence in this new left space, a cat wandering about. This is one of the homes of Left Summit Serbia which brings together many of the left initiatives as well as other civic groups.

We discussed the role of different social movements, including those focused on the recent election protests, and anti-demolition groups, including a quasi-environmentalist one focused on the waterfront 'development' which is called 'Don't Drown Belgrade'. This is an initiative that is part of the 'United Civic Front' which is routinely attacked in the Belgrade press for being small and inefficient (which begs a question as to why the press feels the need to repeatedly undermine it). The anti-demolition campaigns also mobilise in support of residents who have been subjected to forced evacuation from their homes after the transfer of social housing to private companies and the attempt by those companies to ratchet up their profits through various 'development' strategies, strategies that usually, not surprisingly, rely on foreign investment.

The following morning, Tuesday, there was a large successful protest by some of those involved in the OCTOBAR meeting and other groups against evictions of tenants in a working-class residential area of the city. The protests go back to privatisation of housing that took place from 2000 to 2012, the period of what is known as the 'Bulldozer revolution'. The coalition government headed by the Democratic Party together with the right and then, from 2008 with the Miloševićite Socialist Party oversaw a rapid shift to an explicitly market-oriented economy which benefitted war-profiteers, those who were able to make a killing financially from real estate. These ostensibly self-made capitalists used family and party ties with the government to secure access to properties which they then wanted to 'develop'.

One case in point was the Trudbenki construction company which was bought up in 2007 by a member of the Democratic Party who was ex-chair of Belgrade City Council, a company that then quickly went bankrupt after the new owner sold off its assets. The apartments had originally been built by a workers cooperative and were part of a public housing programme, but these needed to be stripped out to realise profit for the new owners. A bank now has property claims confirmed by courts and supported by the state apparatus, with a deal struck between the owner and the bank to evict thirty families and demolish the whole street. There have been numerous threats against the tenants, and they have had to pay huge court expenses already, as well as fines of 5,000 to 10,000 Euros for each household because they live there without permission. This for residents that include pensioners who now receive only 40 Euros a month following government cuts, an austerity agenda demanded by private banks and by the EU. The government is keen to bow to the diktats of the IMF, and is seen by the left as being 'more IMF than IMF'. The protest, which included anarchists and neighbours, stopped the eviction, deterring the twenty police sent over that morning. The bailiff didn't appear, and now the owner apparently has no obligation to send notice of the next eviction attempt. Fascist groups which attack the left and LGBT initiatives are also used by private contractors to beat back civic protests.

Feminism and queer politics was present in Left Summit Belgrade, and is, activists at the OCTOBAR meeting claimed, woven into the fabric of the new movements, and so not necessarily needed to be declared as a separate resource; there was an immediate intuitive resonance with debates about 'intersectionality' that evening. In fact, one of the first national groups in the International Socialist Tendency (IST) to publicly object to the 2013 'Comrade Delta' crisis over sexual violence in the British SWP – the group which effectively controls the

IST – was the Belgrade-based Marks21. Unfortunately Marks21 could not resist putting full programmatic demands to the Left Summit Serbia as a condition for staying involved, and left the alliance when their demands were refused. The dead weight of political traditions often hangs as heavily over the far left as it does over Stalinism. Even so, the group was invited to the OCTOBAR meeting, and were part of the protests against the rigged election.

There is a grim history, but there are, in this difficult context, signs of resistance. There has always been resistance in Serbia, just as there was resistance at the heart of US-American imperialism during the Vietnam war when youth refused to sign up to fight. In Serbia there were over 300,000 deserters from the fighting in the 1990s, and the response to call up to the armed forces was only 50%, and only 15% in Belgrade. When deserters sought refuge in other countries of the EU they were not treated as refugees, but forcibly returned to Serbia.

The struggle of refugees is always a struggle for the rights of the oppressed, and Serbia is yet another case in point. Our struggle for socialism is international, crossing borders, or it is nothing, and it is clear that the new generation of revolutionary Marxists inside Serbia know this. There are now also signs of the development of a political tradition that can draw an honest balance-sheet of the successes and failures of 'socialism' in Yugoslavia and build alliances through which socialism might actually eventually realise itself there.

4

DEMOCRATIC PEOPLE'S REPUBLIC OF KOREA

Three years on from the dramatic structural transformations in Eastern Europe after the Second World War, we shift further east, to Asia, and to a new wave of revolutionary activity that gave rise to regimes heavily influenced by the Soviet Union but breaking from it in order to overthrow capitalism and declaring from the outset that the struggle and the leadership and the economy are 'socialist'.

The DPRK, Democratic People's Republic of Korea, was founded in 1948 in the north of the Korean peninsula after a bloody national liberation struggle against Japanese occupation. The annexation of Korea by Japan in 1910 had been followed by brutal subjugation of the local population, and although those bitter years of colonial oppression were brought to an end with the help of the Soviet Union, the formation of the DPRK was as an independent state led by the Korean Worker's Party (KWP) under the leadership of Kim Il-sung. The local Communist Party apparatus in the years immediately preceding the founding of the DPRK had been directed by

Moscow, in line with the Third International, Comintern and then Cominform policy of utilising local parties around the world as diplomatic tools of the bureaucracy, but was quickly absorbed into the KWP, as were the local people's committees across the north. This was one year prior to the seizure of power by Mao in China, note.

Soviet forces were withdrawn in 1948, and the DPRK was then on its own, despite some continuing trade links and imports of fuel and food, isolated, forced to be self-reliant, an extremely compressed and so impossible attempt to construct socialism in one country. And, worse, only part of a country, the only consolation being that it was the north that was centre of heavy industry with a head-start over the more rural south.

Supreme Leader Kim Il-sung intended Seoul, which is south of the 38th parallel, to be the capital, not Pyongyang, which is to the north of that line. There were uprisings in the south against military rule culminating in a rebellion by the Jeju islanders which was crushed and a dictatorship was established in South Korea under Syngman Rhee, actively supported by the United States. The US henceforth underwrote the regime in the south of the peninsula, and although its own military was formally withdrawn in 1949, covert operations and a build-up of forces preparing for war against the DPRK continued from its base in occupied Japan. The 38th parallel was the line drawn across the country by the US, the new colonial masters in the region after the Second World War, and then transgressed, the trigger for the Korean War from 1950 to 1953, a further ordeal for the DPRK in which much of the material infrastructure was bombed to bits.

Successful defence of the regime in the north entailed further deep costs, not least to the internal structure of the regime.

Defence and closure against external enemies intent on destroying an independent state which declared itself to be socialist, enemies that really were intent on the restoration of capitalism in the north, necessarily led to defence and closure against internal enemies, and so it was that the Democratic People's Republic of Korea took the form it has maintained until the present day.

The Soviet Union had at its disposal the Comintern, the remains of the Third International, to buttress Stalin's own ridiculous anti-Marxist claim to be building socialism in one country, and political-military manoeuvring and then 'peaceful coexistence' were the international conditions for that bureaucracy to survive until 1989. The DPRK did not even have that, and so the illusion of independence became more dangerous, more toxic to the population even when that illusion was fed to its people as if it were a panacea.

Among the consequences of isolation, and as an insidious feedback loop in which the problem is reconfigured by the regime as if it were a virtue, are some weird aspects of representation of the regime both to the outside world and to its own people, a double-edged duplicitous self-representation.

Representation and self-representation

'Mysterious', that's the word for it offered by the Chinese plain-clothes policeman at the northern border. It was meant as a question, and provided as a possible answer to another question he had just posed to a shifty-looking group of Westerners in October 2018 at the small border town: 'Why do you want to go to North Korea?' That it might be 'interesting' as a first answer did not satisfy him. Border security has been tightened in recent years by China, fearful of what the consequences might be if the DPRK regime falls hard, not only because floods of refugees might head further north and to the west but also because the social unrest might also spread, infect and unsettle a carefully managed transition to capitalism guided by Xi Jinping. At the end of the 1990s after severe famine in the DPRK, what is described by the regime as 'The Arduous March', there had been some incursions into Chinese border towns across the Tumen river to the north; some desperate DPRK soldiers had come across, held up households and taken stuff back across the border. China does not want this to be a sign of things to come.

You can only get into the DPRK as part of a carefully-managed tightly-controlled group in which you will be accompanied by two guides and a driver. Even on 'individual' tours, you will be visiting as one of a gang of four. Our group had been briefed in Beijing on what not to do. Don't take photos of the military, and don't take photos of any construction sites because those are administered and staffed by the military. Take pictures of the beautiful scenery, but don't take pictures of ordinary people, particularly of those pushing heavy loads on their bicycles or those working on the roads, for such images could be used as propaganda against the country. Don't refer to 'North Korea', that is disrespectful because the DPRK views itself as a regime in the north attempting to make links with the south, and that means that you should not wear the T-shirt you've just bought, on which the tour company made the mistake of printing an image only of the north of the country; it should have depicted the whole of the peninsula. Take photos of your itinerary because that might be confiscated at customs because the print-out lists key national monuments as if they are tourist sites when, of course, they are no such thing.

Members of the group had already signed a declaration to this effect on signing up, and also agreed not to publish images taken or any written account of their visit before it was vetted and approved. On another parallel tour the same month a hapless Western tourist joined a Chinese group only to be whisked around the Pyongyang monuments on a bus that refused to stop to allow the visitors to get off and have a look around. This poor guy complained and showed the tour itinerary on his phone to the local guide who snatched the phone away and started checking through it. When the group got to their hotel that evening, the lone Westerner was asked by the receptionist to go to a room up the corridor where three men in black suits were waiting for him; they questioned him about why he was there and what his problem was. The interrogation ended with him signing a declaration that he would not speak or write about what had happened to him and then he was invited to fill out a customer satisfaction questionnaire. When he put the wrong answer, a new sheet was put in front of him until he marked 'good, very satisfied' on all the items. Then he was free to go.

We were told not to ask local people, including the local guides, what they thought would happen when Respected Marshal Kim Jong-un, the current leader, died because that would confuse and upset them, and, of course, we should refer to the leaders of the three generations – Kim Jong-un, Kim Jong-il and Kim Il-sung – with respect; not, for example, ever to refer to (I quote) 'fat Kimmy'. The main guide in Pyongyang told us that this was a chance for us to put aside our preconceptions and really see how things were in the DPRK, told that 'seeing is believing, right'. No, dead wrong.

The DPRK is a perfect working example of how ideological systems of rule wherever they are, in the capitalist or so-called socialist world, cannot be so easily dispelled by simply seeing things as they really are; to 'see' here in the DPRK, particularly as a tourist, is to see what is staged. This tourism is no mere façade. Tourism and foreign investment are priorities for the regime, with more resources poured into impression-management than school-education or distribution of vaccines. The service sector now runs at a third of GDP after mining and just above agriculture and fisheries. Most foreign trade, over ninety percent, is with China – minerals and some armaments out, and fuel and food in. I spoke to an INGO, International Non-Governmental Organisation, aid worker back in Beijing who viewed tourists as unwitting voyeuristic parasites colluding with the regime's agenda and effectively obscuring what is really going on. You need some political-historical theoretical grasp of the reality that is being presented to you in order to go beneath the surface, and to go beyond the liberal platitudes served up in smiley crinkly-eyed benevolent BBC travel programmes, Michael Palin's popular 2018 tour east being a case in point.

The visitor circuit around Pyongyang and down to the Demilitarized Military Zone, DMZ, at the border with the Republic of Korea to the south was tightly-orchestrated, a closed circuit. The main hotel for foreigners is a forty-three story total institution with restaurants, pool, bowling and barbers, with restaurants populated only by other tour groups. One of our group bought a new hat with a red star on the front at the DMZ and lost his old cap somewhere along the way, perhaps at lunch. The following morning our second local guide, the minder, turned up on the bus wearing the old cap as a joke and handed it over. It had been retrieved by another tour group from the restaurant where we had eaten lunch, its owner identified and cap returned to our group guides.

On another occasion, second example of the closed circuit, one of our group did a runner. Don't wander off, we had been told back in Beijing, only move around as a group, and if you do wander off it won't be you who gets into trouble but your guides. This guy had already made a break for it on the first evening from our hotel in Hoeryong in the north-east of the country but had turned back after finding there was nothing to see down the dark road leading off into the unknown, turned back to find the search-party guides looking less angry than very relieved. On his second outing during the day-time near a monument we were visiting our intrepid explorer had wandered into a park, encountered some locals, and made it back again before anyone noticed. As if. At our next stop barely an hour later he was stopped by our guides, and his camera examined. He had been spotted, someone had informed the authorities, and he was quickly tracked. It was clear that if we had got away from our group we would not have got far. One of our guides, an older KWP member with some clout among the locals, accompanied a couple from our group back to our hotel by taxi, but only after ten cars had refused to stop on the street and after protracted negotiation at another hotel. Taxi-drivers were unwilling to take foreigners on board.

If we had got away from our group, how would we have talked with the locals? We could have practised choice Korean phrases we had rehearsed together on the bus, which included the rather useless 'Saranghamnida' ('I love you'). We did talk to some school-kids during staged encounters in classrooms, but these were rather limited and closely monitored 'conversations'. Schools and educational extra-curricular institutions were a key selling point on the tour; as one of the Kum Song Youth Publishing House puts in the title of one of its pamphlets, 'Child is King of the Country'. We were told that illiteracy does not exist, which might be true. I asked one boy about twelve years old what he had for lunch and he thoughtfully rolled out a list of dishes, all of the food items he knew the English names for. In another school, four school-girls fourteen years old asked me how popular the British Broadcasting Corporation was. They had been told, and this phrase was repeated to us at least twice by our main guide in another part of the country outside Pyongyang, that the Korean people should 'keep their feet firmly planted on the ground and look over the wall'. They did look over the wall, but what they saw was also filtered in a particular way so that it corresponded with a DPRK-centred view of the world; a common misconception inside the DPRK is that most people around the world speak Korean.

A guide, an older and more trusted working-class KWP member, a more trusted minder than the younger middle-class main guide, told me that he liked Russian films and some English films; the three English films he named were *Bend it like Beckham*, *Titanic* and *Love Story*. Our main guide later said he was surprised that *The Lion King* was not in this top three. The KWP guy told me that there was a nice river cruise in Pyongyang, but he had never been on it. At one point he said he had never been outside the DPRK, though he told someone else that he had been to China fifteen times the previous year. When they were on their own, away from the main group as we walked around a monument or wandered around the country-side and were encouraged to take photos of the beautiful scenery, and when they were drawn into more detailed conversation about their lives, guides looked over their shoulders as they spoke, literally looked around and over their shoulders. There was a double-problem for those of us keen to search out the contradictions, peer through the cracks, try to look behind the scenes. One aspect of this double-problem was the deliberate staging of what we would see as foreground and glimpsed at the edges, and the other aspect was the insidious layering of deception on self-deception, protection of the image of the

DPRK and self-protection of those who might be punished for leaking something else between the lines. We kept in mind two warnings, and you should too.

Deception and self-deception

The first warning is in the Russian documentary about the DPRK available on Netflix called *Under the Sun*. It is, yes, a rather hypocritical exposé from the vantage point of the Putin regime that itself relies on a muddling of truth and lies to cover over its full-blown embrace of the free-market, but anyway what we see in the documentary is a chilling staging of 'everyday life'. It transpires that the father does not actually work in the factory he is shown in, and neither does the mother work with the bemused colleagues she is shown chatting and joking with. The cheap trick the Russian crew pull as they film these encounters is to keep swapping the memory cards in their recording equipment and to keep the cameras rolling between and after scenes. So, we see father giving wise guidance to his workers referring to grading of textiles, and then him being instructed by the minders to specify the cloth weight in more detail. They tell him how. The scene is re-shot. We see the mother being given an award for hard work, and then, between takes, her colleagues being told to laugh more, with more enthusiasm. We see the family having dinner, and the father telling his daughter that she is at a 'good school', and then, as the camera keeps recording, the minder coming into shot to tell him to say it again, but to say it is a 'great school'. When the parents tuck the daughter up at night it is not in her own bed, but one readied for her by the DPRK production team. Seeing is not believing, and it is not even clear what they themselves believe.

The second warning is to be found in the South Korean Suki Kim's 2014 account of working in a Christian college on the outskirts of Pyongyang *Without You There Is No Us: My Time with the Sons of North Korea's Elite*. Suki Kim gets into the college by posing as a teacher, and the college itself keeps going in the DPRK by promising not to evangelise to the students, the crème de la crème of Pyongyang high society being groomed for leadership roles in the regime. This itself is profoundly paradoxical, for Christianity as such is a no-no in the DPRK, the religion practically wiped out after the regime was instituted back in 1948. Pyongyang had actually been a cultural centre for Christianity in Asia, known in the late nineteenth and early twentieth centuries as the 'Jerusalem of the East'. The regime now hedges round this history and its legacy in claims that Christians do participate in one of the two minor political parties, the Korean Social Democratic Party, and tourists are sometimes even taken to a church to prove how open and tolerant things are. The other minor party, the long-standing Chondoist Chongu Party which supposedly brings together followers of Confucian and Shamanist Chondoism, had at one time during peasant uprisings in the late nineteenth and early twentieth centuries more members than the Communist Party and was an important base for resistance to the Japanese occupation. These two minor parties now participate in the Democratic Front for the Reunification of the Fatherland led by the KWP. Other parties did also once contest elections, including one party which represented Buddhists, but these were already hollow shells and have now disappeared.

We visited a Buddhist Temple in mountains in the north-east of the country and a couple of monks wandered around. It was here that we first saw evidence of the increase in internal tourism – mainly wealthy Pyongyangites come to see their country cousins – and they dutifully dressed up in the Buddhist regalia to have their photos taken. At another site a guide had apparently made the mistake of greeting one of the 'monks' as 'comrade', an embarrassing slip which threatened to blow the gaff, to reveal to the tourists that these orange-robed guys are actually dressed up for the part, part of the regime, not really Buddhists at all.

Back to Suki Kim's account of teaching the elite, one in which she becomes increasingly demoralised as it becomes clear that she cannot believe one word the boys say, whether that is about what they think about the regime or what they did that morning. She can see with her own eyes, for example, that they were out on one side of the campus when they tell her they have been somewhere else. In some cases it might be that they simply do not know what the right answer is and are filling in the blanks for a curious foreigner asking awkward questions. There were some awkward moments also for us in the same vein.

We visited a museum in the north-east of the country devoted to Mother Kim Jong-suk, Kim Il-sung's wife, mother of next in line for the leadership, the rather more seedy-looking dark-spectacled Kim Jong-il. We were told by the local guide that Kim Jong-suk gave birth to Kim Jong-il in 1942, and the popular story here is that Kim Jong-il was born in Mount Paektu, the ur-site of the Korean nation celebrated interminably in the ubiquitous song 'We'll go to Mount Peaktu' – the refrain came up from the streets of Pyongyang in the middle of the night, to encourage the workers working on the bridge, we were told, and recurred in every school-child performance, including by the three year old creepy automatons being trained for later work on dance and Karoake shows for tourists in the restaurants.

Kim Jong-il was actually born in the Soviet Union, which makes more sense since this is where Kim Il-sung was then regrouping the liberation forces before 1948. We were then told that his wife Kim Jong-suk died in 1949, a year after the liberation and formation of the DPRK, and we noticed that this was incredibly young, she was 32. Awkward question for the guide; I asked 'how did she die?' and was told, after some blushing and shuffling of feet, that this was 'unknown'. Another guide later answered the question by saying that she died as a result of complications in the birth of Kim Jong-il, but then this would mean she took seven years to die. Look, the issue here is not only the lies as such, not what is concealed, but the very process of concealment. All of the paintings of Kim Jong-suk in the museum showed her smiling, none of the photos showed her so. We could not be sure in what sense the first encounter between Kim Il-sung and Kim Jong-suk was, as was claimed, love at first sight, more or less. It does not, at any rate, look like the marriage made in heaven that is claimed in the state propaganda.

None of the guides knew whether Kim Jong-un, Kim Jong-il's fourth child by one of his lovers, was married or not (he is, to Ri Sol-ju) nor whether he had any children (he has at least one, Kim Ju-ae, and perhaps two others, though it is not clear if these were by his wife). Not a whisper about the wives chosen for Kim Jong-il by Supreme Leader Kim Il-sung, let alone the lovers, and not a hint, of course, about Kim Jong-il's first-born Kim Jong-nam who was heir-apparent until he made a botched attempt to visit Disneyland in Japan in 2001 and met his maker in Kuala Lumpur International Airport sixteen years later.

You won't find this information online in the DPRK because in place of the internet there is a closed-circuit 'intranet', the Kwangmyong. We were shown students busy on computers in Schoolchildren's Palaces and Houses of Study, but they were either working on the smart-art paint-shop software or watching online study programmes. In some cases the kids arrived in the room after us to take their places in front of the screens, and we were invited to believe that they had always already been making use of the generous electronic resources. We were shown foreign-language books available for study, which included *Harry Potter and the Chamber of Secrets* and the *Diary of Anne Frank*. Who chose those books to show us, and who were they hoping to impress?

For the elite things are a little different, perhaps a little closer to what we were being shown, but perhaps actually very different from what we were being shown. Linkedin recently published data showing that that social media platform is still the medium of choice for wealthy North

Koreans, even though they are now migrating from Facebook to Chinese sites like Weibo and Alibaba. Although there is no internet access for the ordinary folk and the poor tourists, and no international phone link outside Pyongyang, there are four different kinds of mobile phone SIM card, one of which will give complete international access to data. That is not for the little people though.

This is the kind of thing that was maddening for Suki Kim in the Christian college. She does not know who or what to believe by the end of her time there. Or perhaps we should not believe what Suki Kim says, and mark her account down as imperialist propaganda. Maybe she is the one telling the lies. You cannot believe what you see or hear, whoever it is who is showing or telling you. Welcome to the DPRK.

Repression and self-control

1948 was a military victory, the DPRK could have been born in no other circumstances at that time, at that place, and the military are at the core of the regime. Questions to the local guides and minders about compulsory military service were also unwelcome, opening out onto awkward silences and a refusal or inability to answer the direct question about how long that service was. Eventually, we were told that that was a 'secret'. Later I heard that it was nine years, and another guide told me that some friends had served two and some had served seven years. A younger guide who was not, it seems, yet a KWP member because he had not done his military service, had escaped it because, he said, if you were a 'genius' you were excused; if you had learnt Chinese or English that would be useful for tourism work – a significant choice of example – it would be a shame, he said, if that knowledge was then lost or was time wasted.

Go to work and get married. We were told that divorce was rare, and difficult, though not so, it seems, for the Kim dynasty. On one occasion, a figure of 0.5 percent was cited for divorce in the DPRK, and this was contrasted with the south where it was, we were told, 50 percent. One guide had a friend whose wife had gone back to live with her mother five years ago, but she had not been able to divorce her husband. The husband had apparently been controlling rather than directly violent. We were told that Korean men are 'intense' and want to be in charge in the home. There are no domestic violence services or refuges. The DPRK authorities claim that the number of rape-convictions per year is in single-figures, so no problem there. This goes against recent Human Rights Watch research which documents widespread sexual abuse by officials alongside general repression.

A foreign aid worker with nearly ten years experience inside the DPRK told me that military service was hell, and this is aside from the network of camps for those who have fallen out of line. The notorious camp in Hoeryong in the north-east has reportedly been closed, but there are others scattered around the country in rural areas. We saw prisoners wearing striped clothing working on the railroad supervised by guards, but then that is not such a big deal if prisoners have been put to work after a fair trial.

There are no lawyers, and questions about legal training were met with incomprehension. You do not need lawyers to complicate the process when you have an efficient justice system. There are no lesbians or gay men in the DPRK, they simply do not exist, they are a Western phenomenon, and so it is unnecessary to have laws against them. I asked about mental health provision. The good news is that there no mental hospitals or even old asylums. The bad news is that when I asked what happened to people with such problems, my question was met with another question, 'prison?'

In all my time in the DPRK travelling through thousands of kilometres of road in the countryside and in cities and walking the streets, I saw only two wheelchair users, elderly men who could both have been honoured war veterans, and no disabled people or with Down syndrome. Difference is erased, invisible at least from public space. An INGO worker told me that services for the elderly are almost non-existent, even if the official retirement age is 60.

There are different internal passports. The right passport will get you quickly waved through the numerous checkpoints in the countryside or through police checks in Pyongyang, the wrong one will see you held up, repeatedly held up. One kind of passport, for Chinese-Koreans, is quite useful now because that not only marks you as a registered minority – this in spite of claims that Koreans constitute a homogeneous pure nation – but as a minority with access to trade networks. Chinese-Koreans, along with the elite – I was shown photos of sleek DPRK citizens in Beijing restaurants –

travel abroad, surf backwards and forwards across the border. Russian as a second-language in schools has now been replaced by Chinese and English. Another passport, for Japanese-Koreans, is more problematic. Those who were lured to the DPRK with the promise of a better life, and as themselves following through on critical reception of Japanese propaganda, understandable reaction to the blatant lies told against the DPRK in Japan, were useful for a while, but now they are suspect, tracked, many regretting the move, displaced and marginalised.

What is Socialism?

In one of the middle schools a group of school-girls almost running out of questions asked me what my favourite colour was. I said 'red'. 'Why?', they asked. 'Because I am a communist', I said. Blank looks, nothing. It was in their living memory, surely, that there were statues of Marx and Lenin in Pyongyang, but those monuments were 'temporarily' removed for refurbishment in 2012 and never replaced. The word 'socialism' still appears in the constitution of the DPRK and in the little books of Kim Jong-un's aphorisms as well, of course, in the writings of Kim Jong-il and Kim Il-sung, texts that cannot be so quickly and easily erased, but Marxism itself has been explicitly replaced, transcended by Kim Il-sung's own guiding philosophy, one signalled in many of the slogans on the public buildings and on the roadsides as 'Juche'. The tallest stone tower in Pyongyang is the Juche Idea Tower, topped with a glowing red ersatz flame, but if you ask what exactly Juche is you won't get any further than a statement that it means 'self-reliance', and if you trawl through the books about Juche on sale in the souvenir shops you are led in circles around the same kind of claim. While Marxism is concerned with the 'material', a guide told me when I pressed for an answer, Juche is concerned with thought. 'So, it is idealist', I said, and she agreed, yes, of course, it is idealist, and so it is.

Juche means that we can do anything if we are self-reliant. This is socialism in one country gone mad. We are not subject to the 'material', but can alter it, and it is 'man' who will carve out a destiny for himself, making the world, the natural and social world, serve man better. The little pamphlet *Juche Idea: Answers to Hundred Questions* published by the Foreign Languages Publishing House and dated the year Juche 101 (that is 2012 Western calendar, that is 101 years after the birth of Kim Il-sung) tells us that 'man is the master of everything'. But there is a twist. If you think of society as being like a giant organism, the pamphlet continues, and this is no mere 'as if' metaphor being evoked here for we are directly told that homogeneous Korean society is an organism, then there must be a 'brain' guiding it. That brain is the leadership, a 'top brain' as the pamphlet puts it. Everything is explicitly hierarchical, top-down.

Some of the stranger formulations by the guides on the coach in the north-east now began to make more sense. They would tell us, for example, that Kim Jong-il 'read the mind of the people', discovered what they wanted, and then directed them to build a road, and so they did, or that Kim Jong-un 'read the mind of the people' and, in line with that, advised them to build a new monument to Kim Jong-il and Kim Il-sung. It is not clear whether the guide really believed this as he said it, and there were moments when he looked a little embarrassed telling us, telling us while the other guide, his minder, a KWP member, watched him. Alongside Juche runs the repetitive ridiculous evocation of Mount Paektu as mythical point of origin, part of the same nationalist ideological package.

You can get into the DPRK as a Christian, as Suki Kim's college outfit clearly indicates and these evangelists are probably playing a long game, but you have to keep shtum about it. You declare what cameras and phones you have at the border as well as what foreign publications you have on you, and you are specifically asked if you are carrying any Holy Bibles. We were told by one foreign guide – and even the foreign guides are accompanied by local guides, remember – that a Christian tour group recently visited, declared their Bibles at customs, had them signed in and then signed the same number out. The local guides were apparently bemused by this, commented that it was downright strange that there was all this singing on the coach about baby Jesus; 'Well', our foreign guide telling us this story, commented, 'I wanted to say, what does that mindless adulation remind you of?'

Juche looks at first sight like a quasi-spiritual belief system, and then it would be tempting to treat the DPRK population as bewitched followers of some kind of cult, attributing their leaders with supernatural powers. That seemed to be the Michael Palin line as he gently pushed his interviewees to admit to some possible faults in their leaders or shortcomings of the system, things that could be fixed, perhaps with a little dose of democratic freedom. Actually, the 'Juche Idea' texts and the garbled repetition of key phrases by the embarrassed guides would rather indicate that it is the kind of belief system that works because everyone is assuming that everyone else plays along with it. It may be no more than that, but no less powerful for that.

Transitions to Juche capitalism

What the turn to Juche as a full-blown alternative to Marxism does indicate, among other things, is that a full-blown transition to capitalism is on the way. The leadership are preparing for this, and, whether they read the minds of the people or not, there are plenty lower down the food chain who are itching for it, even already carving out a space for it. One of the guides discovered that one of our tour group was involved in company research and asked for contacts for foreign investment options to help build a local tourism and hotel business. The same guide also made a proposal of marriage to another member of the group, noting that he very much liked the country she came from, and so he was clearly keeping his options open.

This guy was pretty symptomatic of the rising entrepreneurial middle class. He described his father as a 'businessman', and was puzzled when I was puzzled that there could be such things in a socialist economy. He told me his dad ran an 'import-export' business. For people like this, I was told, membership of the KWP is actually viewed nowadays as rather a hindrance. The good moral standing of KWP members and the careful surveillance and regulation of their lives that goes with it, inhibit the construction of more opportunist networks of money and power, networks that tie the two things together. These two elements of DPRK life are intimately intertwined. Without money in the DPRK there is no power, and without power there is no money. In the DPRK now that is Chinese money, the currency of choice for most business being the RMB rather than the North Korean Won.

Many of the little kiosks along the side of the road and at the base of apartment blocks operating as little corner shops were private enterprises, loosened from state control by oiling their way to greater entrepreneurial freedom of manoeuvre by giving kickbacks to those immediately above them in the chain of command. We were told not to take photos of the large supermarket where middle-class Pyongangites were doing their weekly shop, and there was clearly bulk buying going on, loaded trolleys of goods that would then be taken to other smaller outlets and sold at a profit. There were well-stocked shops in Pyongyang selling a range of consumer goods – in the department store there was a furniture range called 'IKEA' – enterprises that the regime would prefer not be widely advertised outside the country; no photos of that please, we are socialist. We were kept well away from the slums on the edge of the main centre of Pyongyang. I took a photo of a little shop selling kitsch fluffy toys in the ground floor of a large block on the way up to a restaurant and the shop-worker raced out and forced me to delete the photo. The shop was a franchise of a Japanese store chain operating semi-legally.

The existence of private enterprise of any kind was denied when I asked another guide, a KWP member, about it. 'No', she said, there is no private enterprise; these apparently private firms are all, finally, part of the state. And there is some truth in this. There is a loosening of the internal economic gear system, preparation for fuller more explicit privatisation of enterprises, but as yet the decisive shift has not been made. This, while Kim Jong-un makes it clear that the DPRK would like to join the World Trade Organisation and will abide by its rules, rules which we well know will entail privatisation of state organs of production and distribution along with education and welfare services. The question is not whether it will happen but when, how it will happen and how that process will be embraced or resisted by the masses of people who will lose so much when they might think that they are simply gaining more freedom.

Reunification as Temptation and Threat

For all this, for all of the restricted access to the showcase educational facilities that are geared to gifted children, for all of the limitations on consumer choice, this is a political-economic system that has kept going as a space snatched away from the capitalist global economy, maintaining itself longer than did the Chinese regime as a socialised property regime, if not actually socialist, if but a bureacratised parody of what socialism should and could be. It is the longest-lasting non-capitalist space on the planet, and the key question is, when the regime falls, whether it will be to a more genuinely socialist democratic self-consciously organised Korean working class that looks outwards to make international links, or whether it will it fall inward, collapse Ceaușescu-style into a desperate competitive and nationalist grasping for goods, a grotesque parody of capitalism.

The bizarre fantasy peddled by the DPRK leadership is that rapprochement of some kind with the south will make it possible for there to be, as they repeatedly put it, 'one nation, two systems'; capitalism south of the 38th parallel, though this is never actually named as such as capitalism, and socialism in the north, socialism under erasure and already replaced with a self-reliant Juche regime still governed by whoever is the designated 'top brain'. Kim Jong-un, educated in Switzerland and fond of Gruyere cheese, is probably putting his bets on a transition to soft symbolic rule in which there is a shift of balance between power and money, from brute power as such to money as a medium by which one can buy a freer life for oneself and one's heirs.

At the 'mass games' in the 115,000-capacity Rungrado 1st of May Stadium in October 2018, a proud acrobatic and musical display of DPRK history that commemorated 70 years of the regime, one that involved 17,000 Middle-School kids behind the display screens and 100,000 performers, there was a symbolically significant moment towards the end, a culmination point. A giant video image was screened across the side of the stadium showing Respected Marshal Kim Jong-un stepping over the DMZ line that divides north and south to shake hands with

President Moon Jae-in of the Republic of Korea (ROK). What was curious about this crucial element of the display was not that there was applause, but that it was not more enthusiastic, not the ecstatic embrace of reunification that the official narrative would have it. It is quite possible that the toll of the years of separation and the cynicism of a people subjected to quasi-military discipline and surveillance is too heavy now for it to be so easily remedied. There is, I was told by one INGO aid worker, widespread resentment at the elite as well as widespread depression and stress. His bet was that if people had a chance they would string up the ruling family and care nothing about links with their compatriots south of the DMZ line.

This would be a betrayal of the history of struggle that gave birth to the DPRK and to the ROK. Indeed, the achievements of the Korean people in the north have already been betrayed. As Suzy Kim underlines in her 2013 study *Everyday Life in the North Korean Revolution, 1945-1950*, the people's committees across the peninsula functioned until quite late on in the revolutionary process as self-governing organs of popular rule. Those committees functioned at a local level and mobilised the mass of the population in political-educational projects as well as operating as distribution centres under democratic control with active involvement of women on an equal basis with men. The incorporation of the people's committees into the DPRK state apparatus was much smoother than in the south where they were forcibly dismantled and many of the key activists imprisoned. This, Kim argues, helps explain how the DPRK regime gained much more popular legitimacy than the Syngman Rhee dictatorship.

For all of the problems in the north – democratic deficit being the least of it – this must be set in the context of the ROK to the south which has lurched from military regime to military regime interrupted by the April 1960 student uprising, mass protests in 1970 and the Gwangju massacre in May 1980. The war against the Japanese and then the US – the Korean War of 1950 to 1953 – were national liberation struggles that required the overthrow of capitalism and consolidation against all odds of an infrastructure that could now be collectively seized by the people in what would undoubtedly be a dramatic transformation, perhaps, we hope, entailing what Trotskyists have traditionally referred to as 'political revolution' against the bureaucracy.

It is the history of popular protest and democratic self-organisation that links the people of the north of the Korean peninsula with those in the south. Those in the south, temporarily perhaps, now have more room for manoeuvre than their comrades north of the DMZ line. The real revolutionary dynamic for reunification and the building of a genuinely socialist Korea is more likely to come from the south than from the north. Then the top-down Juche system and the ideological veneration of Mount Paektu will need to be swept away in a return to something much closer to the Marxism that underpinned those progressive independence movements in the first half of the twentieth century. A leap into the past will be necessary to really make possible a leap into the future.

5

PEOPLE'S REPUBLIC OF CHINA

This was the next big prize, a huge Asian landmass seized from capitalism that would become the centrepiece of revolution not only in the region but around the world as an inspiration to peasant struggles as well as to the industrial working class, and operating as a counterweight to the Soviet Union, providing some different templates for what 'socialism' might mean but with an ossified leadership that would cruelly betray what it promised.

The People's Republic of China, PRC, was founded in 1949 following a protracted liberation struggle headed by the Chinese Communist Party under the leadership of Mao Zedong, who was chairman of the party until his death in 1976. This liberation struggle had five key elements which are intertwined, but which we need to conceptually disaggregate if we are to make sense of what happened over the next seventy years, if we are to make sense of the nature of the Chinese state now.

The struggle was, first, an explicitly modernising enterprise involving educational projects, battles against semi-feudal superstition, foot-binding and so forth, and continuing in the tracks of the bourgeois-democratic developments in the early years of the twentieth century. These cultural-political developments saw, for example, the emergence of a women's suffrage movement way in advance of many other countries. There was the implantation of ideas from the Western Enlightenment tradition which include those of the idealist philosopher Hegel and, of course the materialist revolutionary Marx.

It was, second, a national liberation struggle, reasserting the independence and pride of the Chinese people against invading forces, most notably, of course, against the Japanese, who had carried out horrific massacres, at Nanjing to note only one of the most well-known examples. The negotiations, and failed attempts to form 'National Revolution United Fronts' with the Kuomintang, entailed bloody failures. The Kuomintang, the 'Chinese Nationalist Party' under Chiang Kai-Shek, butchered communists while negotiating with the imperial powers. It was the Communist Party that emerged as the dominant nationalist force.

The third element, which needs to be untangled from basic national liberation in China in 1949, is that it was an anti-imperialist struggle. The revolution entailed the beating back of the imperialist Japanese invasion forces, and the driving back of the Kuomintang into Taiwan, where Chiang Kai-Shek ruled until 1975; he died a year before Mao. The Kuomintang was ejected from the island of Hainan in the south in 1950, the year that Tibet was formally incorporated into the People's Republic. The British forces, legacy of a powerful colonial presence that were allied with the Kuomintang against the Communist Party, were then beaten back and confined to Hong Kong, and the Portuguese were pushed back and confined to Macau.

With the fourth element we arrive at one of the main political contradictions, which was to provide one of the hallmarks of Mao's rule and of so-called 'Maoism'. This is the rural, peasant-based element of the struggle. There was a contradiction between a Western Marxist emphasis on urban industrial development as the context and motor for communist politics, on the one hand, and the Long March that Mao and his comrades engaged in through the mid-1930s, a long march through the countryside which led them to strategise the struggle as involving the encirclement of the cities. A hallmark of Maoism was to become its praise of peasant struggle.

Finally, fifth, there is a national and international element of what we could call 'rebel Stalinism'; this term to attempt to capture the way that, on the one hand, the Chinese Communist Party was indebted to the apparatus of the Third International directed from Moscow, and, on the other hand, had to break from Stalin's advice. The advice was that the disastrous National Liberation United Front be maintained with the Kuomintang in order to bring about a bourgeois-democratic revolution instead of a socialist one, which, in line with Stalinist 'stage' versions of historical development, would have been premature.

So, the political organisation of the Communist Party was still Stalinist, with top-down military discipline that had been necessary to liberate the country, but Maoism was to emerge as an international force on the world stage with the victory of the revolution. The 1949 seizure of power was a world-changing event. But the world has also changed in the seventy years since that revolution. There is a contradictory process of resistance and adaptation to the international context that needs to be grasped if we are to understand China now and the prospects for Marxism there.

'Marxism' and Marxist Analysis

Leap forward seventy years; where is Marxism in China now? In a peculiar way, the fate of Marxism as a crucial practical-theoretical resource for Mao and his comrades mirrors the fate of Marxism in the advanced capitalist countries; while there are myriad leftist groups, including different competing remnants of the Third International in the Western world, much Marxism as such has been transformed into an academic speciality. It is kept alive in the universities, and that's not only a bad thing, but it is too often enclosed there, and so turned into a scholarly abstract theoretical enterprise instead of a practical one geared to link understanding with political struggle. And so it is in China, where there is occasional lip-service to Marx in public arenas but few statues of Marx or Engels, or even, today, of Mao. You can buy tourist kitsch images of Mao and hammer and sickle souvenirs in the cities, but the one place where you can be sure to find 'Marxism' is in the Schools and Colleges of Marxism deep inside the universities.

And that's what I know of it. I've visited China a number of times over the past fifteen years. I remember the year of the first visit, 2004, because that was the year Jacques Derrida died, something that was cause of some shock and upset among the academics in the conference in Hangzhou, capital of Zhejiang province in the south of the country. I mention it because that conference on linguistics and critical discourse theory saw figures like that, deconstructionist philosophers, as more important than Marx or Marxists.

My most recent visit, in December 2019, was to a more explicitly Marxist context. I was reimbursed by Guangxi University for Nationalities for travel and accommodation, to speak at 'The 46th Discipline Forum of the National College of Marxist Theory Discipline' (maybe it loses something in translation), the subtitle for which was 'International Academic Symposium on' (with the next phrase in scare quotes) '"New Development of Socialism in the 21st Century and Progress of Human Civilization"'. That's what I will mainly describe here, and I'll use it as a peg on which to hang other reflections on what I've made of China in earlier visits.

You need a political frame to make sense of what you are told, and it's this political frame that underpinned my paper at the conference on 'Socialism in the next century', which is probably why it got a polite quiet reception. It is a political frame that includes three moments of analysis from within the tradition of the Fourth International, which was founded in war-torn Europe in 1938, just over ten years before Mao came to power.

This dissident revolutionary Marxist tradition, and an organisation that explicitly broke from Stalinism, is my implicit, and sometimes explicit, point of reference for the debates occurring in China before, during and after the revolution. It gives us three key texts, books that have been influential on me, at least.

The first text is a book by Wang Fan-hsi who died in Leeds at the end of 2002. The book published in Hong Kong in Chinese and then in English in the mid-1990s, is called *Wang Fan-hsi: Chinese Revolutionary, Memoirs 1919-1949*. Wang Fan-hsi was born in 1907, and compiled these memoirs in the 1950s while in exile in Macau. The memoirs trace his political journey from being a member of the Chinese Communist Party in the 1920s. He was a supporter of CCP co-founder Chen Tu-hsiu who resisted Moscow's orders to take distance from the Kuomintang and who was then displaced by Mao, who was a more obedient Stalinist apparatchik. Wang describes encountering Trotskyism during his time in Moscow in the Communist University for the Toilers of the East, and then his return to China in 1929, the formation of the Chinese Left Opposition, imprisonment during the 1930s, and then expulsion to Macau in 1949.

The Trotskyists in China were isolated, caught between the Kuomintang and the Stalinised Communist Party. Along with Peng Shuzhi, who was once on the Political Bureau of the Communist Party (who became a Trotskyist, was imprisoned by the Kuomintang, fled to Saigon after 1949, and then ended up in exile in the United States), Wang was an important figure in the Fourth International, keeping the revolutionary Marxist tradition alive, reflecting critically on Maoism, and paying the price. We can see in Wang's memoirs, and in debates with Peng Shuzhi, questions raised about what Trotsky's theory of permanent revolution meant in Chinese context, and whether they had themselves been mistaken in putting their energy only into urban proletarian movements. In some important respects, Mao was right.

The second text, and it reflects a second moment in the Fourth International's engagement with Maoism, is the Italian scholar and activist Livio Maitan's book published in English in 1976 as *Party, Army and Masses in China: A Marxist Interpretation of the Cultural Revolution and Its Aftermath*. Here in his book there is a history of the revolution, and a balance sheet of the Cultural Revolution which lasted for about ten years, from 1966 until Mao's death, and then the final defeat by the party apparatus of the so-called 'Gang of Four' led by 'Madame Mao', Mao's fourth wife Jiang Qing.

That Cultural Revolution, especially in its first phase, seemed to chime with and inspired some of the 'New Left' movements around the world, reenergising Maoism as a political current. On the one hand, it raised again the question of the peasantry as a revolutionary force, and was an important player on the far-left, along with and often in contrast with Trotskyism, particularly in radical versions of 'Third Worldist' politics that struck a distance from both the capitalist West and the Soviet Union. On the other hand, the Cultural Revolution raised questions about the anti-bureaucratic potential of the mobilisation of the young Red Guards; the extent to which they were being used by one wing of the bureaucracy, that of Mao and then the Gang of Four, and the extent to which there was a dynamic to that movement that posed a threat to the bureaucracy as such, something that revolutionaries should be participating in.

The third text brings us almost up to date, a 2012 book by Au Loong Yu, *China's Rise: Strength and Fragility*. Au describes the fundamental shift in class relations in China since 1949 with rapid industrialisation and the appearance of an urban working class. That working class is divided between those working in the state sector, those working in the service sector, which is rapidly expanding with the production of consumer goods, entertainment industries and new social media, and the role of migrant rural workers who provide cheaper labour living in vast barrack complexes run by large corporations.

Since the 1990s the Chinese Communist Party oversaw two waves of privatisation. Small and medium-sized State Owned Enterprises were privatised first while the larger enterprises were aggregated into joint stock companies. Then urban and suburban land was privatised, something which put more pressure on rural migrant workers who were unable to afford accommodation, even when restrictions enforced by the 'Hukou' household registration system were relaxed. There are thus, Au Loong Yu argues, two forms of capital accumulated and managed and then invested in China now: There is capital which is individually owned by the bureaucrats, figures like Jack Ma, founder of the Alibaba online retail and ecommerce group who is a multimillionaire and member of the Central Committee of the party; and there is collective capital owned and organised according to the needs of the different government departments and regions. There is an increasing flow of capital from one realm to the other, with corruption scandals symptomatic of the too-fast access to collective capital by individuals, and an attempt to rein in competitors who threaten 'social cohesion'. Recently, the inflow of capital from émigrés in Hong Kong and Taiwan has been at least matched by an outflow of capital into the West.

One of the most interesting aspects of Au Loong Yu's book, and his day-to-day work – he is an activist based in Hong Kong, and so is vulnerable to the recent proposals to enable extradition of those deemed evildoers to the mainland – is the fracturing of social cohesion, not only through individual millionaire bureaucrats fleecing the system, but through the many thousands of acts of resistance documented by *China Labour Bulletin*, including mass strikes by rural and urban workers each year. With the recent slowdown of economic growth these have been fewer, and focused on resistance to closures. This has led to two quite different 'critical' responses inside the Chinese Communist Party, with a group of neoliberals advocating full-scale privatisation, protection of private property and 'globalisation' of the economy on the one hand, and, on the other, a left-nationalist current that calls for a more intense crackdown on dissidents and securitisation of the state apparatus.

There has been much debate about 'social credit' as a gathering of data about consumer trustworthiness, but these debates inside the party apparatus could spin the emphasis either on to economic-focused free-market grounds or on to direct political control, of who can access what services and who can travel where. At the moment it is both, which leads Au Loong Yu to suggest that the most accurate characterisation of the system now that it is as a form of 'bureaucratic capitalism'.

Marxism as a belief system

So what do 'Marxists' in the university Schools and Colleges of Marxism make of this, and how do they attempt to justify what is going on?

Well, first of all, Marxism in China is not a political praxis, an analysis that is dialectically and intimately linked to changing the world. On the contrary, Marxism operates as a kind of social glue. In this way, I suppose you could say that it still functions as a political praxis, but one concerned with order rather than change.

Let us take a back-step for an example of this: In 2009 I was at an academic psychology conference in Nanjing where we were treated to the most reactionary mixture of US-American laboratory-experimental psychology – rats in mazes, human beings turned into cognitive-behavioural mechanisms, that kind if thing – and so-called 'indigenous' Chinese psychology, which was basically Confucianism. The Confucius Institutes around the world funded by the Chinese state are a manifestation of this reclaiming of a philosophical system that emphasises the importance of people knowing their place and showing obedient willing submission to their elders and betters, and, as far as Confucius was concerned, of women to men.

One paper in that 2009 Nanjing conference ten years back traced out similarities between Confucius and the French philosopher Michel Foucault. Both, we were told, focused on duties and obligations, and on the way that power relations operated in a micro-managerial 'capillary' manner, linking surveillance with the inculcation of a sense that we needed to speak to those accorded power in a way that maintained power relations. It was an interesting talk, but with one thing missing, which I pointed out; Confucius endorsed and aimed to strengthen these power relations, while Foucault's historical analysis was critical of them, emphasising, in his famous phrase, that 'where there is power there is resistance'. The speaker looked at me dumbfounded, as if that had never occurred to him, and he avoided me afterwards.

During my last visit in 2019 I agreed to teach a session in the School of Marxism at Guangxi University of the Nationalities the day after the main conference. I agreed to do it because I wanted to see what the students made of it. Students from different disciplines, whether from the social sciences or natural sciences, are required to take classes in Marxism alongside their main topic. This is the case in every Chinese university, and this is mainly what the Schools and Colleges of Marxism are up to.

Last year at another College of Marxism in one of the universities in Beijing I asked students who were based in the College, taking Marxism as their main topic, what they would do when they finished the course. They laughed and said, 'teach Marxism'. I asked one of the lecturers, an economist, whether they thought China was capitalist, and they said 'yes, of course it is'. In this 2019 class in Guangxi University, I was co-teaching with another comrade academic, Alpesh Maisuria, a Marxist who had also been invited to speak at the main conference. The Dean of the School of Marxism sat in on the class, and after we spoke about praxis and class struggle, the Dean intervened and said 'we need to learn about Marxism because it is our belief system'. When we had tried to set up the session as a discussion of what they knew about Marxism, the Dean advised against this, saying 'they want to be told'. This had pretty well set the frame for what the agenda was in the main conference, which was to promote, we were told, 'socialism with Chinese characteristics'.

There is an aspect of surveillance and control that makes any attempt to get behind the screen of state ideology in China extremely difficult, surveillance and control that is expressed in forms of management of a visitor's experience of the country. Sometimes that surveillance and control is well-meaning and benevolent rather than deliberate and sinister. The visa application process, now outsourced to a private company, is more of the latter, laborious and intrusive, asking for detailed information not only about where you intend to go, but also where exactly you went last time you visited China. The former, friendlier micromanagement of your time in academic settings, is more common.

At a 2011 conference on contemporary capitalism in Hangzhou, for example, I was told that we would all be taken down to the West Lake for an early evening meal in one of the restaurants. I said that I had stayed in Hangzhou before and would like to follow one of the canal-side paths to the lake myself, and I would meet the rest of the group there. We had been relayed to the conference site, some hours away, from the hotel on coaches early in the morning, and I'd had enough of that kind of mass travel. Our coach driver who had brought us down from Nanjing had a hard time navigating the traffic, and some chaotic cross-cutting of road-lanes, shouting at one point that 'these people drive cars as if they are bicycles'. We had a back and forth argument in which my assigned student guides insisted that this solo walk to West Lake that I was wanting to embark on was impossible, and that I would get lost, it would be dangerous, and so on. I said I really want to walk to the lake on my own, and eventually the penny dropped; they said 'Oh, you need private time', I agreed that it was private time that I needed, and that did the trick. I walked to the lake, went to the wrong restaurant, and arrived at the meal two hours late, causing great panic meanwhile.

The West Lake was much changed since my previous visit seven years before, this is a feeble excuse for my mistake, I know, with private coffee shops, including Costa Coffee, sprung up around the edge, and incredible obvious commercialisation of it as a tourist site. There has, in short, been amazingly fast modernisation of previously quasi-rural parts of the country; skyscraper-strewn cities like Shanghai are now the rule instead of being the hyper-developed exception. And so it was in Nanning, site of the 2019 'New Development of Socialism in the 21st Century and Progress of Human Civilization' conference.

Nanning is the capital of Guangxi Zhuang Autonomous Region in the far south of the country, a 'second tier' city, and so relatively small compared with first tier cities like Shanghai and Beijing; it is about six million strong, a sprawling smoggy metropolis that is known, I was told, as a 'green city'. The campus was quite leafy. A philosophy student who was sent to meet me at the airport – he liked the German romantic (and sometime Nazi) Martin Heidegger, he said – told me that in China there was 'too much development, too many people'. Another student who took over to show me round the Guangxi University for Nationalities campus was more positive, praising the development and modernisation that Marxism had made possible. As an 'autonomous region', Guangxi, which is about the size of the UK, contains a significant minority population, the Zhuang and other groups, whose cultural artefacts are on display in the museum on the riverside, but the name of this academic institution, 'University for Nationalities', has another meaning too.

Nanning is the nearest urban metropolis to the border with Vietnam, and the university operates as a staging post for academic contacts with Indochina, with visiting students from Vietnam, Laos and Cambodia. And here is one crucial link between modernisation, nationalism and a peculiar twist to the anti-imperialist heritage of the Chinese revolution. I will come to that, and the way it manifests itself in debates about 'Marxism' in a moment. Let's turn first to the conference itself.

In the Progress of Human Civilization conference...

There were introductions to the theme of the conference by local worthies, party members, and School of Marxism faculty heads before 'photo time'; visiting guests – that's us from outside China along with Marxism College visitors from other parts of China – sat on chairs at the front and other local speakers stood on the steps at the back. The introductions emphasised what they called 'the integration of Marxism and traditional culture' and links with 'south east Asia' culture, arguing that 'socialism with Chinese characteristics' shifts the balance of power between capitalism and socialism globally. We were reminded that this is the 70th anniversary of the founding of the PRC, and advised that 'during the event our university will provide quality services for you'. One visiting apparatchik from outside Nanning said that they felt 'very excited about the event', telling us that it 'will be recorded in the history of Marxist theory discipline'. What is socialism? 'Socialism is the product of the contradictions of human development' culminating in 'Xi Jinping thought', which provides 'a new viewpoint for world socialism'; General Secretary Xi Jinping shows us that 'we need to provide a Chinese solution to world problems'.

A keynote address before photo time by Professor Song Jin was designed to set the tone for the day (and this was the title of his talk displayed on the screen), 'The Cognitive Logic for the International Dissemination of Achievements in Localization of Marxism in China'. There was a quick run through the history of the Opium Wars, that is, nineteenth-century British imperial import trading of opium against Chinese resistance – the Brits don't come out of this well, to say the least. It was a potent telling reminder that anti-imperialist struggle has a long background history to what eventually happened in 1949. This brought us to the 'contemporary history of China', sideswipes at the Kuomintang and present-day Taiwan, with the lesson that 'promotion or propaganda must run alongside military power'. This 'revitalisation of China' must involve 'the promotion of development theory' and 'telling good stories about China internationally'.

What is to be done? Professor Song Jin said 'we need to win over foreign media' and promote Marxism and socialism, and aspects of that struggle include showcasing 'good research in China'. We build on the observations of Deng Xiaoping, Party Chair from 1982 to 1987, he said, the first of which is the importance of 'development', and the second here is that 'It doesn't matter what colour the cat is as long as it catches mice'. This brings us, as the conclusion of the talk, to the 'three philosophical questions addressed by Xi Jingping, which are 'Who am I, where do I come from, and where am I going?'

After photo time I gave my talk, following which there was no time for discussion, and then there was an extra lengthy intervention by an elderly comrade wearing a grey cap who rambled around a number of different issues before he was told by the chair to wind up; these included reference to the 'failures that can be seen in the Soviet Union', Deng Xiaoping's shift to 'peaceful development', the founding of over 500 Confucius Institutes to promote Chinese culture, 'Chinese soft power' and 'Chinese traditional medicine'. This guy spoke about his visit to Vietnam; 'they made the mistake of privatising land', he said, whereas China has 'succeeded in managing urbanisation'. This was one of the few points in the day when interventions shifted gear from rather abstract distanced commentary on how good Marxist theory was to directly political comments, though these political interventions were just as troubling.

A talk from a Russian academic on 'The Post-Soviet School of Critical Marxism', which was helpfully printed in Russian in the conference book we were handed at the beginning of the day, spoke of 'the tradition of socialism preserved by the great power, China', and then went on to mention some more interesting stuff and theoretical reference points, including Bertell Ollman, István Mészáros, Lucien Sève and David Harvey, though it was unclear how exactly they were being put to work. The 'Post-Soviet School' which has developed over the past 25 years, with Alexander Buzgalin as a key figure, includes focus on the development of global 'late capitalism', 'qualitative changes in the nature of the economy', 'corporate manipulation', the role of 'simulacra' and limits of capitalism. There wasn't time either for the speaker, Olga Barashkova, to elaborate on this, or to do much more than praise Marxist theory in China, invite people to visit her institute in Moscow and look forward to future research links.

At least here we were talking about Marxism as such, but still in a way that was 'about Marxism', and how important that was as a belief system, rather than actually being Marxist as such. Indicative of this distanced relationship to what was supposed to be the central theoretical framework for the conference was a paper included in the conference book by Meng Liangqui from the Nanning School of Marxism on 'Mapping Knowledge Domains Analysis on Marxism in 21st Century' which was using CiteSpace, a software package for mapping dominant trends in research. 'Journal Co-citation analysis' identified key texts in 'Marxism studies' though it is not clear what criteria defined the field, but it included as top 'research fronts' the following top ten keywords: 'Marxism, capitalism, state, politics, history, socialism, globalization, revolution, power, and Marx'.

This kind of list is perhaps what drives the jargon-generator style conference and publication titles produced by the Colleges and Schools of Marxism. The top five text resources from the 'co-citation analysis' were *New Left Review, Capital, Antipode, Historical Materialism* and *Theory and Society*. Top author citation counts ranked in the top five, Marx, Marx (so he got the top two slots), David Harvey, someone only identified as 'anonymous', and Antonio Gramsci. As regards top documents from the citation analysis, these were Gramsci's *Prison Notebooks*, Marx's *Capital*, Geörgy Lukács's *History and Class Consciousness*, Michael Hardt and Toni Negri's blockbuster *Empire* and, fifth, Ernesto Laclau and Chantal Mouffe's *Hegemony and Socialist Strategy*.

This is interesting not so much for what the analysis throws up, but for what the point of the analysis is and the role it plays within 'Marxism Studies' in China. We know that Chinese academics over the past years have been assiduously tracking what the key debates are in Marxism and have been translating key texts into Chinese. Until recently these texts have only been available to the party cadre, but the work of the Schools and Colleges of Marxism in each university indicates that the texts have now been so successfully enclosed within academic space that they no longer pose a threat. These texts no longer need to be explicitly restricted to the cadre because the university is effectively sealed off from the population.

Our participation, we Marxists from the West flown in to an academic conference, is obviously part of this phenomenon. What could we possibly say in this context that could be a threat? We were being used, and we knew it. In any case, the dominant language of higher education being English has further insulated the population from possibly dangerous subversive ideas. We know that some young scholars in these university-based institutes have been punished and, in some cases, been arrested and disappeared after putting the ideas they have been reading about into practice. Demonstrations by Marxist academics in support of the 2018 Jasic Technology strikers, for example, have been violently suppressed.

It was now becoming clear that there was to be no time for discussion after the papers, and what little wriggle-time there was would be plugged up with unscheduled speakers, now Professor Xinping Xia who followed up on the Russian talk by speaking about the way the Russian School was borrowing from Chinese Marxism, and then, a weird indicative sideways move, about the functions of the Chinese Army in protecting the development of socialism. There were aspects of these extra interventions, where the speakers spoke without notes, that felt, especially through the simultaneous head-set translation, like slow rap; the ideological preoccupations of the moment were coming into the head of the speaker and blurted out into the conference. This particular speaker went on to describe the publication in Russian of an 'Encyclopaedia of Chinese Spiritual Culture', and the importance of Confucius as 'an organic part of socialism with Chinese characteristics', of 'traditional culture'. It was good, he said, that 'the Soviet Academy' was more open than the West to the rational nature of China's success rather than simply treating it as an inexplicable 'miracle'.

The other British speaker, Alpesh Maisuria, was more successful than me in keying into some of these preoccupations and to the theoretical level of the conference, speaking about the importance of alleviating poverty and the way that neoliberal capitalism relies on mystification, making it seem that communism is no longer feasible. Then we were quickly brought back, in another unscheduled intervention by a visitor from Hainan Normal University, to a brief review of and praise for the Russian Post-Soviet Critical School, warning that 'critiques of the Soviet Union that focus on Stalin have some Western themes'.

This brings us to the significant strategic location of Nanning and the Guangxi University for Nationalities; it was telling context for a talk from a Vietnamese academic and another from Bangladesh. These talks were also sandwiched between extra interventions, which again squeezed out any time for questions and discussion. Pham Thi Chauhong began by tracing the origins of democracy to ancient Greece, its development in the thought of Marx and Lenin, and then the role of the Vietnamese Communist Party, VCP, in promoting 'socialist democracy' which blossomed in 1986 with the 'collective ownership for the labouring classes'. After 1986, she said, the VCP has protected 'peoples rights and interests'; 'we improved inner-party democracy' and 'leadership efficiency', rectifying, for example, the 'balance of power between prosecutors and courts' and acknowledging the role of competition and entrepreneurship which are 'popular issues among youth', moving to a 'market-oriented economic system with socialist characteristics' which includes attention to 'cyber-information security and development of e-governance'. A lot packed in there.

The talk by the Bangladeshi speaker was more interesting and indicative still. The speaker, Mostak Ahamed Galib, was not actually living in Bangladesh but working in the School of Marxism in Wuhan University of Technology. The son of a diplomat in Beijing, he had remained in China. His paper was on 'The peaceful rise of China through "Belt and Road" initiative with a special focus on people to people partnership'. The Belt and Road Initiative, also known as 'One Belt, One Road', comprises road and rail and sea trade routes through six 'economic corridors' which link China to the world, and that link developing countries directly to China through infrastructure development loans, the infrastructure for which is designed to increase trade.

We were told that the Belt and Road Initiative now involves, six years after it was announced by Xi Jinping in 2013, 138 countries as a 'cooperation platform' and as a 'welfare centric initiative'. You get the picture so far that there was not to be a whisper of doubt about any of this, and in fact the intervention at the conference was focused on rebutting criticisms of it. The main criticism is that it draws other countries, including Vietnam, Laos and Cambodia, but also way beyond, into a 'debt trap', with strategically important countries provided loans which then mean that they are in debt to China. We do see this around the world, including in Latin America.

No, this is far from the case, we were told, and the guy was shouting into the microphone now, because what the Belt and Road Initiative does is lift 7.6 million people out of extreme poverty, and the loans are taken out as a 'free and open contract'. This is, he said, 'a win-win cooperative project'. Again, no questions or discussion, but afterwards when I pressed him on this, he admitted that there had been problems with some of the loans so far, but that this was because Chinese entrepreneurs who didn't understand local contexts had made some 'bad deals'. This was, he said, very different from what Xi Jinping intended, and rules were now being tightened up, with more training for state-owned and private enterprises.

This contract model of the Belt and Road Initiative driven by 'development' and profit imperatives illustrates well how China, from being resistant to imperialism, is now up to its ears in it, part of imperialist penetration of capital and commodification into every corner of the world.

This was all of a piece with the message that came through in the other papers after lunch; that development was bound up with China being able, as one speaker put it, to 'stand up', 'enrich the people' and 'make the country stronger'. Another speaker, Professor Chen Yuan, asked the telling question as to whether it is possible to avoid capitalism, and argued that 'Chinese socialism' has not escaped capitalism, but that we need to think again about the historical order between capitalism and socialism if we want to find 'a new direction for human civilization progress'.

Another speaker gave his paper very quickly in the afternoon, apologising that he had to leave early to travel back to his own university because he had a 'performance review meeting' the next day. I felt for him. I had resisted pressure from the conference organisers to take long flights with multiple stops to arrive on Saturday in time for the Sunday conference and leave China to go home on Monday. I have the sense from talking to Chinese academics that the pressures on them there make the complaints from Western academics about their own workload pale into insignificance. The world of an academic is of a piece with that of hard-pressed, suicidal party apparatus bureaucrats.

There were now briefer talks, these in Chinese, eight minutes each, about 'global governance' and the 'ecological sense of being as part of Xi Jinping thought'; 'ecologically', we were told, 'we need to improve the environment'. There were complaints that China was being blamed for CO2 emissions when actually the problem was the result of 400 years of development in the capitalist countries, fair point, and so the burden should be shouldered by the capitalist countries. This would be a 'crisis transfer' way of dealing with the problem. Confucius and 'traditional Chinese culture' was evoked again a number of times, as was the importance of 'coordinating Chinese language with the world'; 'we should tell good Chinese stories'. Is Confucius socialism, one speaker asked? No, says Xi Jinping, and so we need to clarify what traditional Chinese culture is, and regard it as 'socialist Chinese culture'. If we want to break through 'traditional thinking', someone else said, we need to 'criticise ourselves', combat 'wrong ideas'. Yes, one speaker said, there was corruption, but that could be addressed by changing the mindset of the leadership and 'old and backward practices', replacing these with 'evaluation criteria for inputs and outputs'.

There was to be no time for debate, everything seemed stitched up. Alpesh Maisuria and I complained bitterly about this at lunchtime, and convinced the organisers to open up a space toward the end of the afternoon session for what they called a 'Q & A' which would replace the coffee break. (The morning coffee break included biscuits and cakes and bananas and mandarin oranges and fresh lychees, product of this sub-tropical region of the country.) This is where a surprising eruption of politics into academic debate occurred. There was a good deal of heat in the discussion around one of the short papers that had been given late in the afternoon which had the title 'Revalorization of the Chinese Nation and Tranquility'.

The argument of the paper went as follows. The historical suffering and liberation of the Jewish people could have lessons for China, raising a question as to whether they, the Jewish people, could be liberated as 'Jews' or as 'human beings'. The Jewish people were isolated, and isolated themselves, the speaker said, and their liberation was through asserting 'Jewish ideology' by establishing the state of Israel. We could learn from this, for 'it threw light on Chinese people and revitalization of the nation'. In the additional Q & A session, there were many objections to this narrative, but mainly on the basis that the history of the Chinese people was entirely different, and their national identity forged through anti-imperialist struggle could not be reduced to that of another different people. There was some discussion of the problem of Zionism as itself an ideology that could be oppressive to the local population, Palestinians, something I pointed out, but this was quickly skirted over, and we moved into the closing talk on, you will be amazed to hear, 'socialism with Chinese characteristics'.

...and out in the city

Translators always have something interesting to say about meetings they are brought in to work at, and this was no exception. Alpesh and I posed for photos with the translators when the conference was over. The translators said they were a bit anxious about the quality of their translation into English, which was actually really very good, and they apologised that they had not had sight of the papers in advance, only being brought in very late on, arriving that morning and expected to launch into action.

The translators had to work freelance, and, with background academic study in politics and languages, they were forced to compete not only with the state enterprises but also with a proliferation of private companies that employed people and offered translation services at impossibly low rates to organisations. Academic organisations like the School of Marxism in Nanning were expected to outsource its work. This was privatised precarious zero-hours work.

Alpesh commented that during our visit to the city centre the previous day we had not encountered any homeless people. The translators smiled and said that this was probably down to what they called 'urban management'. There are gated communities in Nanning, as there are in Beijing. Travelling out to the edges of the very efficient clean new metro system to the south, north and west of the city, I could see different kinds of community. In some cases, those estates near the university, they were more typically middle-class, while at the edges and in the south of the river centre away from the shopping malls these were enclosed poorer spaces with checkpoints. At the farther south edge of the city were timber yards and shacks where workers and their families lived with farm animals.

Shopping malls in Nanning were, as in Beijing and Shanghai, glitzy consumer heavens housing the likes of KFC and Starbucks. Around the local mall area close to the university there were cheaper open-air restaurants in the car-parks, and in one of these there were pictures of Mao on the wall, a rare sight, and a reminder not only that such imagery is not so common now, but also that to display such pictures must indicate some decided political choice on the part of the owner, a reminder that there are still such decided political choices, one of those permitted by the regime.

Closed-circuit cameras are everywhere, and we know that there is sophisticated face-recognition technology in the urban centres that enables the authorities to track the movements of the population. This is not at all peculiar to China. Social credit surveillance, for example, is actually already present in Western capitalist countries. It is a function of capitalism, and an indication of how far and fast China is travelling, and in what direction. Regime-friendly justifications for social credit include that Chinese citizens positioned as consumers are happy to buy into it.

There are still spaces in China where this kind of surveillance is not necessary. When I was able to get out to the edges of the city on the metro I then walked in near-countryside. As evening draws in, the flash of the cameras is more evident back in the city, more intrusive, a reminder that everyone is watched, or is reminded that they may be watched; this is surveillance culture in action. The time for pedestrians on the zebra crossings to get from one side of the road to the other, by the way, was just a little less than necessary; the car is becoming ruler of the highway and the highway routes define the shape of the city.

Western Development

China is a successful capitalist country, success built through a revolutionary break with its history of dependence on imperialism, and on a reassertion of its national independence through the unifying force of a party apparatus that was itself built with the help of a foreign power. Marxism itself is part of that heritage of Western Enlightenment and developmental modernisation, but now absorbed and harnessed to the needs of the state, as have been the rural forces that made the revolution, absorbed and harnessed to a rapidly urbanising country.

In the process, the contradictions of which Marxism speaks, class struggles, are displaced onto the notion of 'development' as such, an ideological process which conceals, seals over, the real contradictions that are still present, and which are actually intensifying as a gap widens between the super-rich at the head of the party apparatus and the rest of the population. The repetitive claim and justification that this is quintessentially Chinese is as bogus as any other nationalist argument for exploitation and oppression. It will be necessary to work at every contradiction in the ideological apparatus as well as in the workplace to being Marxism to life again.

Every radical social movement, ranging from those that make claims for their own national identity against the Chinese state, as in Xinxiang, to the #metoo and LGBT movements, and including a nascent trade union movement, are present in China now. That will put pressure on the 'Marxists' confined to the universities to make a connection with the real world, a process that revolutionary Marxists around the world should play some part in, in debate and in solidarity.

6

REPUBLIC OF CUBA

We shift continent, from Asia to the Americas, for the next act of resistance to imperialism a decade on, now in the backyard of the United States – the area that it often designates as such – and a revolution that grows over from democratic nationalist tasks in such a way that actually really puts socialism on the agenda; this both for those taking part as they seize the means of production and take control of their lives and for those watching across the rest of the continent who will be inspired to take such a step themselves.

Cuba is a 'unitary Marxist-Leninist one-party socialist republic'. That is what it says in the constitution, and that official designation needs to be taken seriously in any evaluation of Cuba's place in the world, and where we place ourselves in relation to it. A victorious liberation struggle was led by Fidel Castro and Che Guevara at the head of the July 26 Movement, J26M, named for the date of an unsuccessful attack on the Moncada Barracks in Oriente province in the east of the country in 1953. The J26M succeeded in chasing out military dictator Fulgencio Batista at the end of 1958.

1959 was the year everything changed, not only in Cuba, where a wave of land reforms, expropriation of land and takeover of large cattle estates went way beyond what many of the local and expatriate financial backers of J26M expected, but also in the wider world. The United States quickly reassessed the cautious support it had given Castro the previous year while it was trying to disentangle itself from Batista's obviously corrupt and unsustainable regime, and the Soviet Union came into the frame as an alternative source of support, as supplier of petroleum that Cuba desperately depended on, and as customer for the sugar that made up over 80 percent of its export industry. Castro promised compensation to the US-based sugar companies, to be paid out of the revenues from sales to the US, a canny move that sent a clear message to Cuba's old masters barely 100 miles to the north at its closest point, so close, so deadly. A deal was signed early in 1960 with the Soviet Union – sugar for oil – and through 1960 there was nationalisation of sugar mills and refineries, and of electric power and telephone companies. By the end of the following year, 1961, Castro declared himself to be a 'Marxist-Leninist'.

While 1959 was the hinge-point for the transition, from the Cuban revolution being a national-democratic rebellion against US control and against its local puppet leaders to being something more recognisably socialist, the following three years – 1960 to 1963 – were crucial in shaping Cuba as it is today. Banks, both US-owned and locally-owned were nationalised in 1960, as were all remaining US businesses shortly afterwards. Guevara, who had brokered the crucial sugar for oil deals, was now in charge of setting up new trade deals with China, and began steering the internal financial reorganisation of the country as President of the National Bank, while trying to manage Cuba's relationship with the Soviet Union and China.

Cuba was caught politically between two versions of Stalinism, needing the two powers for economic survival and necessarily, inevitably perhaps, accommodating to the demands placed by each bureaucratic leadership, mainly with that in Moscow which at one moment sought status from links with revolutionary anti-colonial movements and at the next sought to contain those movements in order to safeguard diplomatic relations with imperialism. Peking was a dangerous counterweight to that, dangerous to the revolutionary left, no more democratic, less powerful on the world stage but with more prestige in the so-called 'third world'.

J26M was merged with the student Revolutionary Directorate and the Popular Socialist Party in 1961, and in 1963 the United Party of Socialist Revolution was formed, accompanied by a purge of nearly half the membership. These years, seeing attempted invasion by the United States at the Bay of Pigs in April 1961, the missile crisis in October 1962 (a standoff in which the Cuban government had no say over what was being threatened and negotiated between the two superpowers), and the US blockade lasting to the present day, are when the shape of the one party, officially re-launched as the Cuban Communist Party in 1965, the one that now governs this island of little over 11 million people, was forged.

Today it is not sugar but tourism that is touted by the regime as a key economic driver; President Miguel Díaz-Canel declared in early 2019 that every tourist to Cuba is breaking the blockade, a blockade tightened by the Trump regime following 60 years of pressure, sabotage, terrorist attacks and assassination attempts designed to bring Cuba back into line as a client state of imperialism. More than half of Cuba's food comes from imports, and now it must also import tourists. Guevara, murdered in Bolivia in 1967, and Castro, who died in 2016, may be gone, but the regime is still searching for new ways to circumvent the blockade as something that functions not only as a political-economic choke-hold on the Cuban people but also symbolically as an isolation device, threatening to enforce the impossible idea that only 'socialism in one country' can be, and must be, constructed here; an island of socialism in a sea of sharks and crooks intent on getting their property back, getting all property back into private hands.

Cuba is a case example of the way international context, the balance of forces in a world that is still capitalist, now more intensely and triumphantly hostile than ever to socialism after the transition to capitalism that took place in Russia and then China, enters into the political organisation and everyday institutions and the mindset of those who support and of those who oppose the regime in this enclosed trapped space. Every step forward, every step towards reform, and every attempt to adapt the country to the changing balance of forces is marked by the consequences of isolation. The consequences are practical, direct restrictions on what is available and how people can live and how they are materially divided from each other. It is also ideological, about how the Cuban people, and we who would wish to build solidarity with what remains of what became a successful and enduring anti-capitalist revolt against the US in its backyard, make sense of this, how reality is filtered. What we see when we are there is filtered by that contradictory play of forces, and filtered for a visitor even before they arrive.

The Continuing Propaganda Offensive

First filter, for visitors, comprises the competing images of Cuba as anti-capitalist and anti-imperialist icon and of it as state-managed top-down authoritarian regime. We know that; we know that there are those competing images, but what is worst is the way this filter is reconfigured in the tourist guide-books, the most insidious of which at the moment is the *CubaConga 2019* 'underground guide'. This is an excellent place to begin, actually, for the guide neatly pits itself against the bland 'introductions' to Cuban reality that the most popular travel handbooks dish up, and it plays into the suspicion that those other handbooks are playing safe. All information about Cuba, it warns, is 'tainted', and worse than that, 'nothing is as it seems'. *CubaConga 2019* plays on the motif of the video game – the reference in the title is to the 1980s arcade favourite Donkey Kong which spawned the Mario series – promising to raise the visitor up to level 5 while warning them that they will never make the top level. This because under 'tropical communism', we are told, life is one big scam; every Cuban will be out to scam you, just as they scam the system and each other. No one in Cuba really works, nothing works, and you better get ready to be treated as what the Cubans call a 'yuma'; a 'yuma' is a visitor, gringo or not, waiting to be squeezed of their money, and all the better if they can be shared, in which case they become what is known locally as a 'punto'. In this way the visitor is launched into a paranoiac journey where they will distrust everything that is told them and everyone they meet. The *CubaConga 2019* guide exemplifies the operations of 'fake news', feeding suspicion, with the message 'nothing is what it seems' seeming to undermine ideology while simultaneously reinstating it, discrediting each fact in the name of revealing the facts to be simply elements in the game.

Once we are in this paranoid universe, one that is antithetical to any solidarity that the visitor may feel for Cuba, every disconfirmation of the handy information this guide offers is further evidence that nothing is what it seems; the game has simply been quickly upgraded to fool the player. But I will tell you anyway that; when the CubaConga guide informs you that you can only buy roadmaps of Cuba in the departure lounge of Havana Airport, that is a funny fact, but incorrect; that none of the owners of the 'Casas Particulares' – licensed bed and breakfast home-stay accommodations – we stayed in were 'elite' members of the Cuban Communist Party intent on stopping you from talking to ordinary people, unless they were good liars; that you will not be made to pay extra car service costs by state rental firm Havanauto on your return to the airport, in fact our car, a bit ropy with a weird tiny battery, was fixed twice free, and then we were given a replacement car; that you will not be overcharged in hotels and restaurants, every bill was accurate, in some cases effectively rounded down. This even in taxis after we had been warned by locals that you should take care not to be squeezed, and taxis were organised by them for us – something *CubaConga 2019* would tell you is the sure sign that you will be squeezed again – and were in line with the agreed fare. In one 'cafeteria' near the north-west coast, the hot old woman owner of the tiny house showed us her medicines, complained about her health and climate change, but didn't want to charge us for the coffees. Some people were reticent, more about that in a moment, but it was not at all a case of having to read between the lines but being prepared to have open conversations when it was possible and listen to what people said.

Twenty years ago, 1999, my previous visit to Cuba, was toward the end of the 'Special Period', an awfully difficult time in the 1990s after the collapse of the Soviet bloc, when the sugar and oil agreements were ended, as was all other aid, aid that was necessary to counter the effects of the US-led blockade. The country was just beginning to pull itself out of economic hardship and, in some cases, hunger, hunger that was only alleviated by the ration system. Twenty years ago, yes, I got badly ill after eating in an illegal home restaurant when driving down the battered bicycle and donkey-strewn highway to Santa Clara and Trinidad de Cuba south-east of Havana, and I was hassled to give the guy who found accommodation with a freezing cold shower more money afterwards. But where have I not been treated as a money-tree and shaken down by poor people, something that is quite understandable. I am from the West, after all. In some parts of the world a network of tourist police cracks down on this kind of thing, intensifying oppression and exploitation rather than addressing it. Is that what you want? This time out to the west of Havana, both in areas near the coast where there were few tourists and inland where there were more, we were given gifts of local food to see us on our way, we were not 'squeezed'. What contradictions there were, were in the main more open and transparent than they are under full-blown neoliberal capitalism where the scam-element is woven into every promise and delivery of a good or a service.

Money as Medium and Obstacle

The second practical-ideological filter on the visitor experience comes into play in the very real division between the two currencies (a division that is now being re-evaluated by the Cuban government). For visitors to the country there is the CUC, the Convertible Cuban Peso which is directly pegged to the US Dollar, one for one; and for the locals there is the Cuban Peso which currently runs at about 25 to a dollar. The CUCs have images of monuments on, and the Cuban Pesos have images of famous figures (the 1 with Jose Martí, the 3, rarer, sold on the Havana streets to tourists, with Che Guevara on it).

This currency division effectively divides the country into two layers. The first layer is the state-organised economy, the bedrock of the political-economic basis of the revolution that was laid down in 1959. It is at this level that the rationing system works, works well. A small quota of milk, sugar, flour, coffee and other essentials are available at very low cost. This ration system continues today; in one simple ration centre, the guy sweeping the place up at the end of the day invited us in and showed us the table of goods and prices. Children and pensioners will get basic goods free of charge. So, the actual cost of living in Cuba is about a third lower than in the UK, and rent is nearly 80% lower. The pay is low, and seems at first sight lower still when it is calculated in the Cuban Pesos in which it is paid, but then the cost of accommodation is incredibly low, and education and health are, of course, free. A basic level of housing, social and welfare support is thus provided. The remaining Cuban Pesos can be set aside for 'luxuries', but this currency is actually useless for anything beyond housing, collective transport and the local restaurants. For that you need to have access to the CUCS.

It is those who have access to the CUCS who circulate in the second layer, the one in which tourists experience Cuba most of the time, and this monetary division often goes alongside geographical division. There are visitors who now travel outside Havana into the countryside, especially to holiday towns like Viñales to the west which are often packed with Western day-trippers spending CUCS, and some who hire cars, but this is still unusual. Several times we were asked, with some astonishment, why were not in Varadero, spending our time, and money, in one of the all-inclusive beach resorts. Life with the CUCS is effectively more like life under neoliberal capitalism, where there is precarious and sometimes lucrative employment; to rise from the world of the Cuban Peso into the world of the CUCS is to touch the tourist economy and to function as part of the service sector, from which come the images of 'yumas' and 'puntos'; here, as under capitalism in any other part of the world, things and people are turned into commodities.

One taxi driver told us that he used to work as an engineer, and got 1000 Pesos a month, but then shifted over to tourist work because he got better paid, and he then had access to CUCS. Owners of Casas Particulares may not be CCP members, but they are lifted away from the rest of the population through their access to the CUC economy. These CUCS are valuable, for what they signify and for what they can actually buy. At La Roca restaurant in Havana – an old cheap state-run restaurant with an old slow jazz orchestra playing to a small audience of diners – we handed over a 50 CUC note, which was then passed up from the waitress to the cashier and then to section manager. There was a tiny nick out of the corner of the note, and so it was returned to us, refused because, we were told, the overall manager, when they saw it, would refuse it.

At the currency exchange at Havana's José Martí International Airport on my way out of the country the woman in front of me in the long queue to change CUC convertible currency back into Western currency again was a Cuban woman. She was not travelling, but had come in to the airport just to change money, from US Dollars into CUC. We waited for nearly an hour before it was her turn to go to the counter. She handed over five

Dollars, one of which was refused because there was a little tear in the note, and came away from the counter with four CUC.

The Manufacture of Dissent

The third filter is an unavoidable one which separates out the life-world of the tourist from the world backstage. You see the signs for the operation of Committees for the Defence of the Revolution, the network of CDRs that have formed the local backbone of the revolution since 1960, but you don't, of course, see how these work. Glimpses of their representative and sometimes coercive function are but that, glimpses. There were advantages to hiring a car and driving the pot-holed country roads away from the main tourist centres, and there were many disadvantages to long journeys in battered cars on difficult terrain. Hitch-hikers were grateful for a lift.

One woman we picked up near Bahia Honda way east of Havana was travelling, she said, to her church in the next village. Cuba now defines itself as a 'secular' state rather than as atheist, and though Jehovah's Witnesses have had a hard time – banned from organising in 1974, and so about 3,000 left in 1980 from Mariel Bay, a time when those who fled were referred to as 'gusanos' (worms) – there are still Roman Catholic churches and, increasingly, evangelical Pentecostal churches, for one of which our evangelical hitchhiker on this occasion was a worker. The Roman Catholic church claims that 60% of the population are of their flock, though actual attendance is between 1 and 2 percent. This woman said that in her part of the country things were pretty evenly split, among believers, between Roman Catholics and Pentecostals. We asked her what her work was, and she said she worked as a teacher for her church. What did she teach? 'The Creation!'

There is still Santeria, Afro-Cuban local religion from the old slave times, with competing stories about whether this was celebrated or dissuaded by the CDRs, probably both. And there were competing stories about Jews. We were told by one opposition activist, for example, that most of the Jews had left the country after the revolution, some to go to Israel, some to the United States, where there are now specific ethnic Cuban-Jewish communities. But we found an active synagogue in Havana, and we were told by a Lebanese family-background maintenance man in one Casa Particular on the edge of Havana that, no, there was an extant Jewish community, but they kept out of politics. This guy also told us that after the revolution he had to give over the top floor of his large family house to homeless people, but he didn't complain about this, accepted it as part of the process of fair redistribution of resources he was then living through. We were told that there were some converts to Islam, and that there had been some fights between Sunni and Shia in the streets recently. Among the opposition there is also some contempt for the progressive shift made by the Cuban government under the impact of HIV/AIDS to active support for LGBT rights (something that pits the government against the Catholic Church), and contempt for the quite good, not perfect, public policy and information campaigns against sexism and racism.

In Viñales on the main stretch there was a brightly painted Freemasons Hall, open, it said, on Saturday morning at 9am. This is a reminder that the freemasons were the guild organisations of the bourgeoisie, progressive at one point in our history as the bourgeoisie replaced feudal rulers but reactionary now in the West where capitalism is entrenched and the freemasons remain dedicated to its continuing existence. In Latin America, where the bourgeois independence struggles came later, the freemasons played a progressive role within living memory, and key figures like José Martí and Simon Bólívar were members. Remember that the Cuban revolution was a bourgeois-democratic revolution against US imperialism that then had to grow over into socialism in order to carry out the basic bourgeois-democratic tasks; it was an instance of 'permanent revolution'.

There is some suspicion of the CCP but not, as you might expect, a sense that membership is necessary to advance through a career or to get special privileges. In fact, despite Castro's decision, after the death of Guevara in Bolivia – death which followed brave if mistaken attempts to extend the revolution through 'foco' guerrilla warfare – to put in place financial incentives, and despite the selective distribution of television sets and other electo-domestic goods to 'vangard' party members in the 1980s, there is still not a privileged class layer of the population in anything like the same way as exists outside the country (whether in the remaining Stalinist states or in the capitalist countries). We spoke to young lecturers in Havana University who shrugged their shoulders as they told us that while the average wage is around 1000 pesos a month for skilled workers, it is 600 pesos for academics; but why not pay those who have worse jobs more money? These young academics were rather distant from the regime, pointing out the private restaurants to us that were, they said, much better than the state ones. When we asked them if they were members of the CCP, they said that, no, the party was for old people, something quite evident in the televised reports of meetings on the television. But when we asked them if they thought they should join the CCP, they said, no, they had never felt it would be a disadvantage not to be a member, so no point joining. As for Marxism, if Marxism meant falling in line with the 'Sino-Vietnamese' model much vaunted by the regime at the moment, then, no, they were not Marxists, they said, but if it meant that one could be critical while supportive, then that was another question. The big battle in the Department of Philosophy, they told me, was over changing the title of the degree, which was actually a general degree in philosophy, so that it would no longer be designated a degree in 'Marxist-Leninist Philosophy', a title that was a millstone around the neck of any young academic who then wanted to go and study elsewhere.

A sprightly woman in her seventies, not the owner of a Casa Particular, told me that she had been a student activist before the revolution, an exciting time, she said, with continuous perilous activity that she enjoyed very much. We asked her if she was a communist because she certainly talked like one. She said no, but then elaborated a detailed narrative for why this was so, one that was at one with the revolution she had lived through, not against it. Yes, she remembered that in the early years of the revolution, time when there were still armed counter-revolutionary groups engaging in sabotage, she had heard the noise of gunfire early in the morning in Havana as opponents were seized and shot. The death penalty was restored in Cuba under the new regime. This woman was not a member of the Cuban Communist Party, but the reason she would not call herself a communist was because this was surely, she said, a state of being to be aimed for, not one that we could or should imagine to be achieved, and not simply with a party card. I was reminded of Che Guevara's rather moralistic injunctions to the Cuban people to work harder to build socialism as a function of aiming to build what he called the 'New Man', not to rely on material incentives. An office building Guevara oversaw the construction of did not, apparently, have elevators because, he argued, it was better that office workers get some exercise climbing the stairs.

There were, in the early years, immense political differences between the three different organisations that were brought together first into the Integrated Revolutionary Organisations, in 1961, then into the United Party of Socialist Revolution two years later and then into the Communist Party of Cuba, which was founded in 1965 and which had its first congress ten years after that. Castro and Guevara's J26M had, of course, been forged primarily in the peasant struggle, and it needed to link with the student Revolutionary Directorate which was based mainly in the towns and in Havana, which was then and still is the largest city in the Caribbean. And J26M needed a disciplined organisational resource base that was to be found in the Popular Socialist Party which had been founded way back in 1925 as the local communist party, section of the Third International, and so tightly controlled by Moscow.

Here is the internal local root of the problem that Cuba has faced from the beginning, a root of the problem of Stalinist bureaucracy that was intertwined with the Soviet compact. It should never be forgotten that the Popular Socialist Party, PSP, actually supported Batista right until the last moment, opposed the Havana General Strike that was called to support the J26M guerrillas in the countryside, and that it tried to put the brakes on the nationalisations that turned Cuba into something like a workers state. There are three elements of this direct local influence of Stalinism on Cuba that gives to Cuba both a bureaucratic and a deserved 'Radical Face of Stalinism' and which Castro and Guevara, at times, fought.

The first is the political apparatus that J26M lacked, and which it needed in order to be able to govern the country. The twists and turns of the PSP as it followed one disastrous line given by Moscow to the next had the effect, as with other communist parties that were franchises of the Third International, of hardening the organisation, making its leadership all the more obedient while all the better placed to give orders, to enforce top-down administrative rule.

The second element of the direct local influence of Stalinism was the commitment of the PSP and then the continuing Stalinist apparatus inside the CCP from 1965 to a 'stage' notion of historical-political development in which the 'national democratic' stage must come first, and only then can the 'socialist' stage be advanced. In countries dependent on imperialism, as Cuba was dependent on the United States up until 1959, that meant that the Stalinists opposed the revolution growing over from carrying out basic bourgeois democratic tasks by engaging in socialist revolution. We are still not there yet, but this revolutionary space is blocked, distorted, waiting its moment to flower again.

The third element is the classic distortion of Marxism expressed in Stalin's notorious phrase 'socialism in one country'. Here in Cuba it means not merely an attempt to cope with the brute reality of the situation, to make the best of the isolation the country suffered, and then to attempt to break out of that isolation (as Guevara tried to do in the Congo and then, fatefully in Bolivia), but to twist the narrative into celebration of this isolation. The celebration of socialism in one country not only leads to nationalist distortions, something that Cuba has bravely challenged – with an internationalism that is also, then, tangled in the manoeuvres of the Soviet bureaucracy, but an internationalist spirit nonetheless – but also to a concordat with other regimes around Latin America and around the world that call themselves socialist but are not, and with others that would not even claim to be so.

Together these three elements have enabled hard-line pro-Soviet forces inside the regime to sometimes gain ascendency, and for Castro, after Guevara's death, to wobble between critique and praise of his Soviet ally; this leading him, for example, to endorse the Soviet invasion of Czechoslovakia in 1968 – a turning point for Cuban foreign policy – and to condemn Solidarność in Poland in 1980.

The symbolic re-framing of Cuba as if it were merely another iteration of Soviet rule can be seen in documentary films such as the 1964 *I Am Cuba*, a film that is effectively unravelled in interviews and quasi-semiotic analysis by the 2004 Brazilian documentary *The Siberian Mammoth*. Inside Cuba, despite the 'Marxist-Leninist' tagline in the constitution, there are busts aplenty not of Marx and Lenin, but of José Martí, a revolutionary democratic leader of the movement for independence from Spain who was killed by the Spanish in 1895. In a case of history repeating itself, this first time in Cuba as tragedy, we might say, the movement Martí led was actually 'annexationist' rather than 'secessionist'; his aim was to break from Spain and attach to the United States. In the first round repeat performance during the Cuban revolution of 1959 we see the regime surviving by breaking from the United States and ending up in hock to the Soviet Union.

The isolation that has distorted and even, if some analysts are to be believed, 'deformed' this worker's state from day one, is welcomed by those who would wish to crush the life out of anything remaining of the revolutionary hopes of late 1950s. Owners of the Casas Particulares said that business was bad with the tightening of the blockade by Trump, with a sharp decrease in numbers of visitors from the United States, and we could see that many of them were empty. But for those who are intent on bringing down the regime, an increase in hardship is the price worth paying, and would even be better because it would also result in more dissatisfaction with the government.

We had a long conversation with an opposition activist, the son of a friend who had left Cuba, who made it clear that for him the blockade and Trump's recent pronouncements about human rights were good things, at last the opposition had an ally in the White House, this in contrast to the tentative links that Obama had made with Havana. Trump tells the truth, we were told, and, when pushed, this guy said that although it would be bad, although it was not what he wanted, he would go so far as to support an invasion by the United States, because, he said, they, the regime, 'they are killing us'. He was against the recent election of López Obrador because that would relax blockade pressure from Mexico, and against the recent pension and ration and minimum-wage increases because that would mean that the population would be more contented with the regime.

There was also delighted support by him for Jair Bolsonaro's reference to the Cuban doctors as 'slaves'. We knew that medical training is a big thing in Cuba, and not at all the elite specialised technocratic enterprise it has become in so many parts of the so-called developed world. A Mexican friend's son training to be a doctor had elected to do his placement in Santa Clara, for example, and he described how the lack of up-to-date medical equipment – the lack a function of the blockade – actually meant that doctors were trained to feel and interpret the body. Their expertise really was hands-on, and the treatment was geared to the lives of the patients rather than to the needs of the large pharmaceutical companies. Medicine was geared to health rather than to profit. One of the hitch-hikers we picked up was travelling with her niece to the small town of La Palma to do shopping and, she said, to buy medicine. Her niece would, she said, be enrolling in medical school in Pinar del Rio, the nearest large city, but it didn't seem a big deal. This woman was otherwise quite scornful about local provision of services, but medical training was taken for granted as something that was available to everyone. There has been a huge outflow of medical expertise and of development of medical training; 400,000 medical professionals working in 165 different countries since 1960, and 31,000 students from 103 different countries coming to Cuba to be trained in its Latin American School of Medicine since 1998. Life expectancy in Cuba is currently 79 years, high given the conditions it has been exposed to by its neighbour to the north for daring to defy it.

The doctors working abroad are 'slaves', according to Bolsonaro, because the Cuban government draws up the contract for them to work abroad, obtains 4,000 pesos a month, and then passes on only 1,000 of this to the doctor. But the contract is quite clear, and the doctor chooses to sign up, and the wage they send home is good payment. Our opposition activist would have none of this, pointing to the difficulty that the doctor then had in breaking from the contract, or returning home to be with their family in case of domestic crisis, illness or death. This is true, and there is a degree of bureaucratic monitoring of the population that is uncomfortable. It is true but clear, unfortunate but understandable in a country still effectively on war footing against the United States.

When we asked our oppositional activist friend what he thought about Trump and Bolsonaro, he said he didn't care; all he cared about was, in a mantra relayed through the Madrid-based online paper *Diario de Cuba* from the US state department, 'freedom of association', 'freedom of movement' and 'representative democracy'. Yes to freedom of association – that is happening in effect with access, from 2019 to the internet and instant group social media messaging, and yes to freedom of movement, but 'representative democracy' where those with the most money have access to propaganda tools turns democracy into a market-place with a corrupt layer of 'politicians'; then we really will be in the world described by *CubaConga2019*. One owner of a Casa Particular complained that their kids were now spending their time playing games on the internet. What the guys who wrote *CubaConga2019* do not reflect on is the fact that the metaphor of the Donkey Kong video game expresses perfectly the condition of life under capitalist fake democracy; everyone is encouraged to scam everyone else in the field of politics. For the oppositional activist, it was as if, in a message in reverse, we had the true meaning of what 'socialism in one country' means. This was 'reaction to socialism' in one country.

Here is a paradox. We were told that people cannot move freely around the country, and there is a particular problem for those who would want to relocate their families or find work outside their home town. Dervla Murphy's typically idiosyncratic 2009 *The Island That Dared: Journeys in Cuba*, a book which was commended by the British Communist Party paper *Morning Star* in the UK (a reliable barometer of Stalinist solidarity sensibility), doesn't pull its punches on the bureaucratic pettiness that can mark some encounters of ordinary people with the system of rules, rules that are sometimes inflexible and harsh, sometimes relaxed and humanised. For example, despite the oft-repeated claim that people outside the tourist convertible economy are wary of interacting with foreigners, we found ready takers for offers of rides in our car from village to village, and we heard from locals who complained bitterly about the state of the roads, and laughed contemptuously when we asked what local representative body they might talk to in order that things might be put right. When it came down to it, the complaint was about lack of resources, lack of goods, and lack of medicines, effects of the blockade.

A woman asked us to let her out of the car just before we arrived at the town she was aiming for – she was there for her fortnightly shop – and was quite clear that this was because she needed to check into the police station to register her presence there for the day. She said she would rather walk along to the police station than have us drive her there in case questions were asked. We dropped her and watched her as she popped in and out of the police station and then carried on to do her shopping. Perhaps she also told the police about us, who knows.

An older woman, not a member of the CCP, described to us the ethical dilemma the blockade posed for her. She, not incidentally, was someone who tactfully talked about Cuban friends who had chosen to live abroad, neither referring to them as 'gusanos', as was once the way at the time of one of the many mass exoduses permitted if not encouraged by the Cuban state, nor referring to them as 'mariposas', the wonderful wealthy creatures who returned home later. (8% of the population, of which many were middle class professionals in addition to the very wealthy and the crime gangs who ran the casinos and brothels, left in the years after the revolution.) There were, this woman said, medicines available for her outside Cuba, and so, because of the blockade, unobtainable. If she thought about this question as an 'individual' question – as one concerning only her own rights to the medicine – then she might feel sad and even bitter about it, but if she thought about this as a collective question which made evident the plight of the Cuban people as a whole facing unfair sanctions for taking back their country under their own control, then, no, that was an entirely different matter.

Solidarity from the Right and Left

Human rights cannot be reduced to basic provision of food and education, as some more hard-faced Stalinist supporters of every twist and turn of the regime will make out, and revolutionary Marxists should insist that more opportunity for critical political critique is the pre-requisite for better social organisation, not a hindrance to it. However, it should be remembered that the political-economic basis for human rights is exactly what is being attacked by the imperialist powers circling Cuba. Trump and Bolsonaro do this in the name of 'Human Rights', and so we need to be clear where we stand on this. Those political-economic gains of the revolution need to be vigorously defended, gains which include, note, that infant mortality in Cuba is now lower than it is in the

United States, that over half of Cuban MPs are women, the second highest proportion in the world, that forest cover in Cuba is now up to 30% compared with 11% before 1959, and that diseases have been eradicated in Cuba that are beginning to reappear in other parts of the world afflicted by poverty and corruption.

It is astonishing that Cuba has survived, so close to the United States and so all the greater threat to the oppressed there who might dare to take back into their own hands the wealth they had created for the few. It has been under pressure of the blockade which denies the basic trade links that are the lifeblood of a globalised world, under pressure from the Soviet Union to imitate its own bureaucratic forms of rule, and then more isolated through the 'Special Period' and collapse of Soviet aid in the 1990s. It has come through all this to the current oil-dependent relationship with Venezuela, a capitalist country where the regime is clinging onto power and also faces invasion threats from the United States.

Solidarity with Cuba as a revolutionary break from imperialism would be easier for us, for revolutionary Marxists, if our own Trotskyist comrades had not taken such bizarre political positions during the crucial years at the beginning of the 1960s and if the Cuban leadership had not fallen in line with some of the worst Stalinist caricatures of Trotskyism. The Trotskyist POR(T) were followers of Juan Posadas, issuing ultimata to the regime to move fast and then, incredibly, urging the Soviet Union to unleash a worker's 'Atomic War' with a first strike on the United States. This delirious twist on the 'defence' of the workers' states was, of course, a threat to the regime.

Guevara, for his part, first defended the 'comrade Trotskyists', but then defended the smashing of the printing plates for a copy of Trotsky's 1937 very relevant classic *The Revolution Betrayed*. Guevara had a copy of Trotsky's *History of the Russian Revolution* in his knapsack when he was caught and killed. Against this background, it is all the more understandable, if regrettable, that Castro should denounce Trotskyism as counterrevolutionary, a line taken direct from the Stalinists. From these contradictory indications as to the political leanings of the Cuban leadership also flow some of the more ridiculous notions in the Trotskyist movement; that Castro was an 'unconscious Trotskyist' on the one hand, or that there could not have been a revolution because there was no revolutionary Trotskyist party leading it on the other. This double-failure, a political failure of analysis and leadership at crucial moments since 1959 has then led revolutionaries themselves to oscillate between starry-eyed enthusiasm for the regime and over-harsh condemnation that chimes with imperialist attempts to destroy what remains of this beacon of hope.

Earlier in 2019, before our visit, there was a Trotsky conference in Havana – good – a positive event, but at the same time the organisers made clear that they wanted an 'academic' debate, and they did not want this to lead to the little sects arriving and trying to set up their own franchise groups on the island. External quarantine leads inevitably to internal quarantine. When I asked the young lecturers at Havana University – they were interested in alternative approaches to Marxism, doing theses on the work of one-time Trotskyists Perry Anderson and Terry

Eagleton – they said they had never heard of the Trotsky conference.

Of course the Cuban revolution faltered, it could not do otherwise, but in this very incomplete imperfect process there exist the grounds for hope that the revolution might be extended, as it must be in order for Cuba to survive. The blockade will either be lifted in such a way as to allow US-American capital to flow in and for property to be re-privatised, for the misery of life under capitalism to return, with massive wage and status differentials. Or the blockade will be broken through active support for the Cuban people in such a way as to also resist the encroachment of imperialism in the country. This is not going to be an easy task, and we need to know what fault-lines are for such solidarity.

That is where the debates about whether it is really 'state capitalist' or a 'deformed worker's state' examined by John Lister in *Cuba: Radical Face of Stalinism* come into play. Whatever the precise political-economic diagnosis, what is most alive in Cuba is the inspiration it gives to revolutionaries outside. This was possible here, something was possible, and such a thing might be possible again somewhere else, in many places, for there to be two, three, many Cubas. International socialist solidarity and action for Cuba is crucial if the revolution is to become something real for us all.

7

LAO PEOPLE'S DEMOCRATIC REPUBLIC

We had to wait over a quarter of a century before the next wave of revolutions rocked capitalism back in Asia, this time as a direct consequence of resistance to imperialism during the Indochina war, during which time China operated as the linchpin of struggle, at times assisting and at times restraining the peoples of Southeast Asia, and the bloody desperate nature of the protracted struggle left its marks on the kind of 'socialism' that could then be built out of the rubble.

Laos is the size of England but with about a tenth of the population. The seven million people there have bravely fought invaders and oppressors, and suffered a history in the last half century or so that saw about 10 percent of the population murdered by the US military. The Lao people fought alongside the Vietnamese in the Indochina War, and then, with the defeat of the US in 1975, the Pathet Lao seized power, ruling the new Lao People's Democratic Republic, LPDR, through the Lao People's Revolutionary Party, LPRP, ever since.

Bounded by Vietnam, Cambodia, Thailand, Myanmar and China, this land-locked country is clearly open for business, and under intense pressure from its neighbouring states, as it has always been. The capital is Vientiane, a relocation of the administrative centre from the Buddhist temple complex of Luang Prabang, both of which suffered from invasions and levelling of religious sites over past centuries by the Vietnamese, by the Burmese, by the Thais, and then by the French and the United States.

The history of the most recent bloody struggle is still very much present, still claiming new victims day by day. Laos is, for the size of its population, the most heavily bombed country in the world, an incredible two million tons of bombs were dropped on it by the US between 1964 and 1973. Many of those bombs were targeted at the areas around the Ho Chi Minh Trail which runs down the country next to the Vietnamese border, and the Johnson and Nixon regimes were able to deny involvement for many years while US military bombing runs decimated the population (literally 'decimated' it). US planes on missions across Laos would also often offload remaining weapons on their way back to base over other parts of the countryside in order to save themselves the risk of landing with live munitions on board.

Thirty percent of those bombs dropped on Laos failed to explode and they are now under the surface, often in the form of small cluster bombs the size of a tennis ball, and sometimes as complete bomb casings. There are 300 casualties a year from 'UXO', 'unexploded ordnance', and an unending task of tracking them down. The murderous legacy of imperialism which had profound effects on the shape of 'socialism' here is heart-wrenchingly portrayed in the 2007 Australian documentary *Bomb Harvest*.

Opening for business

The first advertisement over the walkway from the plane in Vientiane in January 2017 is for apartments in a gated community. Enclosure and privatisation are the watchwords in Laos now.

The most detailed history is by Grant Evans in *A Short History of Laos: The Land in Between*. A revised expanded edition of his 2002 book appeared in 2012 shortly before he died (by which time he had become enrolled as an academic advisor and member of the Lao Academy of Social Sciences). The book was published in Thailand, not in Laos. Grant Evans was former editor of the Communist Party of Australia newspaper *The Tribune*, and so makes some astute political comments about the pressures the Pathet Lao were under before they took power in 1975 and then the machinations of the LPRP as it renegotiated its relationship with the Vietnamese Communist Party, the Thai regime and with China. Evans doesn't shy from the issue of prison camps set up after 1975 nor from the racist revenge treatment of minority communities that were doubly unlucky, their people oppressed and then enrolled in the US military's dirty war.

From 1978 to 1979 the government, egged on by Soviet advisors (of which there were about 1,500 in the country by that point), undertook a disastrous agricultural collectivisation programme. The programme was cancelled within eighteen months after regional authorities had produced local returns showing that there were nearly 2,500 collectives formed. Part of the problem was the resistance by local farmers, and the problem was compounded by the bureaucratic nature of the exercise; local officials were keen to comply with the demand to collectivise, but they did this by simply reporting inflated numbers of collectives to impress their superiors rather than actually doing anything with them on the ground. Agriculture and forestry counts for about 43 percent of production, industry and construction about 32 percent, and the growing service sector, which includes tourism, counts for just over 25 percent.

The regime has its eyes on foreign investment but is always the junior partner. For example, the front page story of the 9 January 2017 *Vientiane Times* was that 'Four foreign companies ink deals for use of Lao satellite', but it turns out that China, one of the countries that will lease the satellite, actually designed, developed and delivered it into orbit. This is a Private Finance Initiative in which Laos pays China, which controls the technology, and then China makes use of the product. The same issue of the newspaper has more glowing reports about energy generation, one of the growing industry sectors in Laos, which aims to complete industrialisation, undergo its own industrial revolution, according to the government, by 2020. Electricity now accounts for over 10 percent of exports in vast hydroelectric projects, including the 2010 Nam Theun 2 dam coordinated with China and Thailand. Garment output accounts for just over 13 percent, and timber nearly 16 percent. Copper and gold still accounts for over half of exports, and the private companies responsible are the most lucrative legal entities in the country. The timber export figures are particularly unreliable. The army was told to make itself financially sustainable in 1988, and has set up a number of private partnerships, many of which are illegal; there are vast areas of the country that are no-go zones for visitors guarded by army personnel functioning as paramilitary protection forces for logging operations that then smuggle hardwoods out of the country. Ecology in Laos is a site of struggle.

This problem of deforestation was documented by the observant traveller Dervla Murphy back in 1999 in her book *One Foot in Laos*; she feared then that the situation was getting worse, and it is. There were parts of the countryside she couldn't access, prevented by local town chiefs and militia, and she was warned that it was dangerous because of remaining guerrilla operations by disaffected minority ethnic communities, particularly the (H)Mong who are still distrusted because of the role they played during the Indochina war, then mobilised by the US forces for counterinsurgency activities.

There is some truth that these guerrilla forces were indeed a threat, and a prominent right-wing counterinsurgency battalion commander, Vang Pao, active in the country before 1975, was still aiming to overthrow the government at the time Murphy travelled in Laos. There were attacks around that time on government forces; even, in 2003, attacks on tourist buses on Route 13 from the capital to the old capital Luang Prabang, attempts to undermine the regime. However, with readjustment of US foreign policy, and Obama's 2009 declaration that Laos (as well as Cambodia) was no longer Marxist-Leninist and so no longer a threat to the free world, these remains of the counterinsurgency have pretty well evaporated.

Some activists from the émigré (H)Mong community in the US were arrested a few years back for planning a coup in Laos, a message to them as to where US interests now lay. Even Vang Pao saw the writing on the wall, and sent a message from exile on 22 December 2009 that 'we have to make a change right now', and proposing peace talks. A Lao Foreign affairs spokesperson replied, reminding him that he had been sentenced to death in 1975, and pointing out that any peace talks could only take place after the sentence had been carried out. Vang Pao died in January 2011. There are still old anti-communist voices, of course, and whether the Trump regime will be more sympathetic to them than Obama remains to be seen, but it seems unlikely.

In fact, it transpired that the main danger to Dervla Murphy during her travels came from state and para-state forces guarding illegal logging operations. Murphy also described the development of new highway schemes that, alongside the dam projects which displace local minority communities and the logging and mining operations, are 'industrialising' the countryside in accordance with the private profit imperative. Murphy can be accused of romanticising traditional rural life in Laos – a criticism that has been made of her other travel books – but she is quite right about the problems with the way this particular kind of industrialisation is taking place. For example, the 13 January 2017 *Vientiane Times* reported on its front page that the go-ahead had been given by the Vientiane People's Council for a new highway that will cut along the edge of the city next to the Mekong. The artist impression image of the road shows toll-booths, and even this newspaper – a private enterprise that also effectively functions as a government mouthpiece – reported over the following days the fury of local residents who were being told to give up land in return for a cut of the profits from what was explicitly being sold as a 'Public Private Partnership'.

Privatisation apace

Vientiane Times copy is vetted and, as 'Big Brother Mouse', the NGO literacy project points out, all books have to be approved by the government before publication. There are innumerable corporate control mechanisms to manage different civil society organisations that might pose a threat to the regime; Buddhist groups are registered and monitored by the state, for example, and Christian organisations have to operate under the auspices of the 'Lao Evangelical Church'. There are no democratic institutions. In the 133-member National Assembly elections for the Lao People's Democratic Republic, voters choose from 190 candidates selected by the Lao People's Revolutionary Party. These 190 include four 'non-party' candidates from the 'business sector'.

When the phrase 'Public Private Partnership' is used in Laos it is necessary to keep in mind that state sector employment has never been more than 1 percent (whereas it is roughly 23 percent in the UK and 14 percent in the United States). Conscription and the operation of local militia forces organised by the LPRP ensure the state apparatus runs without having actually to employ many people. What might easily be assumed to be state concerns, such as the ubiquitous outlets for 'Beer Lao', a quite nice lager made from rice, are actually all private; Beer Lao is made by Carlsberg, and the nearest competitor, pissy 'Namkhong', is made by Heineken.

The regime moved very rapidly after the first glimmerings of glasnost, faster than many other regimes in the Soviet sphere of influence and behind the 'Bamboo Curtain'. Explicit private finance initiatives were already in place in 1986 with the announcement of the 'New Economic Mechanism' – the final abandonment of any official claim to be building a socialist or, still less, communist country – and in 1988 Laos opened up to foreign investors, shifting its focus from the Soviet Bloc to Thailand and then to capitalist China. This also meant loosening ties with Hanoi, and the remaining 45,000 Vietnamese combat troops were withdrawn from the country between 1988 and 1989. The LPDR withdrew support for the Thai Communist Party, hinted at repatriation deals of émigré activists with Bangkok, and this did the trick in facilitating new economic ties to the south, to Thailand. These possible extradition arrangements now extend to activists with the Thai Red Shirt movement. After shopping their old comrades in Thailand, the way was also open for deals with China (over extraction mining and hydroelectric dams).

China repatriated 3000 Lao in 1997 that had been retained by it up to then as potential guerrilla irritants to the regime were they to be needed, and Jiang Zemin visited Vientiane in 2000, the first state visit by a Chinese premier to the country. A train-line between Vientiane and the Chinese border is on the books, and land enclosures have begun to seal off areas of land and remove local inhabitants to make way for it. Photo-shoots of trade deals on the LPDR websites now show images of pudgy Lao government ministers in crumpled suits rather awkwardly shaking hands with their sleeker flashily-dressed Chinese counterparts.

There is a growing new middle class that races around in massive shaded-glass SUVs and which is linked to and protected by the regime. For example, the holiday town of Vang Vieng is popular not only with Australian, European and US back-packers but also with the wealthy kids of the apparatchiks in the capital. Most of the hotels are ranged along the right bank of the Nam Song river, but the left bank has become site over the last few years for unofficial restaurant sites which blare out heavy beat music through the night. The right-bank hotel owners petitioned the local mayor, who sent a letter of protest to the regional authorities to be forwarded to the capital. The left-bank rave sites were driving away guests unable to sleep through the noise, ruining their business, but the hotel managers have no recourse to the state. They cannot ask the local police, they said, because the police never act without a bribe, and in this case the police are reluctant to take action against the left-bank noise-makers because they are the sons and daughters of wealthy families in the capital linked to the regime.

The opening up of Laos for business, and correlative abandonment of any pretence of its aim to build a socialist society free of imperialism, has also been accompanied by the return of old ideological forms. For example, after 1975 there was an attempt to institute new forms of egalitarian nominations of identity. In place of the elaborate speech codes which respected and reproduced class and caste hierarchies, the regime promoted the use of 'sahai' (or 'comrade') as a form of address. A businessman back visiting Laos who had fled the country for the US in 1975, complained, while travelling on the bus from Vang Vieng to Vientiane, that things had changed in the country under the new regime, even that the language had changed so much that, he said, about seventy percent of it was now unrecognisable to him. What had been lost, he said, was the 'depth' of the old language, by which he meant that the markers of respect and contempt so that you know who you are speaking to in the chain of command weren't now present in everyday speech. But things are changing again. The 'sahai' form has all but disappeared now, with 'than' (or 'sir') making a comeback, and also the 'nop' (the respectful bow of the head to superiors) returning.

Many grim returns

Kaysone Phomvihane, leader of the Pathet Lao, died in 1992, and there were attempts after 1995 to build a personality cult around his image, but these attempts have failed. Memorial sites around towns with busts of Kaysone (busts manufactured in North Korea) have fallen into disrepair. It has been other statues of leaders that have been venerated with offerings of flowers on significant anniversaries instead, leaders like the historical royal personages Fa Ngum and Chao Anou, but also the more recent figure Prince Souphanuvong who worked actively with the Pathet Lao against the US but who marks some kind of lineage with the old monarchy deposed in 1975. Wealthy figures from the regime will now even appear in public as benefactors for hospitals or youth centres, making donations to good causes, symbolically re-enacting the monarchical forms they were supposed to have abolished.

A ceremony in December 2002 for the erection of a statue of King Fa Ngum (1316-1374) was attended by state officials, who clarified that this was not intended to signify, they said, 'the revival of the monarchy'. Nevertheless, this event and the denial itself does indicate something of the way the regime is now stabilising itself. This stabilisation also entails recomposing relationships between the nation state and religion. Laos is a Buddhist country, but the monarchy was Hindu, with strong traces of Hindu imagery in Lao Buddhist temples. If a new monarchical regime of any kind is to re-emerge it will be on the basis of a new compact with the Buddhists.

The Pathet Lao and then the LPRP directing the LPDR had historically strong connections with the Vietnamese, with many inter-marriages in the course of the anti-colonial struggle up to 1975. That too is changing. Today it is rare to find leading figures in the party or state apparatus with Vietnamese partners, and there are rumours that it is difficult to obtain a powerful position in the economy or government if you are not 'pure Lao'. (H)Mong youth in a literacy class in Luang Prabang complained of their marginalisation by the Lao. The Lao youth who participated in discussion wore full orange Buddhist robe.

Diverse opposition

There has been opposition to the regime since 1975, and not only from the disgruntled remains of the US occupation forces (of Vang Pao and the like). A 'Social Democrat Club' in Vientiane was formed and then rapidly suppressed in 1990. The Vice-Minister for Science and Technology, Thongsouk Saisankhi, complained that the LPDR was a 'communist monarchy' – a telling diagnosis of the problem – and called for a multiparty system. He was arrested and died in prison in 1998. In 1999 there were student protests in Vientiane which were violently suppressed. Since then, and with the fading of insurgent activities by the (H)Mong and other 'tribal' peoples, opposition has tended to shift to the NGO sector, to a quieter practical building of alternatives around questions of ecological sustainability and food security. But even these are dealt with viciously when they start to intrude on interests of corrupt private-state enterprises.

Environmental activist Sombath Somphone was abducted in 2012 on a street in Vientiane, and hasn't been seen since. His work in the Participatory Development Training Center that he founded continues. The complaints about his disappearance are bitter but cautious. Sombath's wife Shui-Meng Ng, who still directs the project and works in the Saoban craft shop in Vientiane, emphasises that the work was not designed to be a critique of the regime but was on the basis of peaceful engagement with community issues. Dervla Murphy makes the interesting claim, in some of the later interviews reported in *One Foot in Laos*, that the matriarchal character of Lao culture has meant that while the male leadership of the state has collaborated with big business, the development of alternatives more in line with the original collectivist ethos of the Pathet Lao – a communist anti-imperialist and environmental ethos – is kept alive by the women in the apparatus organised through the Lao Women's Union. Murphy's book provides a more ecological and feminist account than Evans' *Short History of Laos*, a good counterpoint to it.

The LPDR state flag (a white circle on a blue central blue strip edged top and bottom with red) is often accompanied by the LPRP (Pathet Lao) red flag with a yellow hammer and sickle emblazoned on it. So, there are symbols of the old socialism around aplenty, but little if nothing of the practice. The suggestion that Laos is a 'deformed workers state' or, more bizarrely, that, with China, Cambodia and Vietnam, it is one of four 'socialist' countries in the region is laughable, insulting to the people of Laos as well as to any historical political analysis of what is actually the case, damning with faint praise. One of the hotel managers in Vang Vieng shrugged hopelessly at the corruption of the local police apparatus and the futile petitioning for something to be done to protect their businesses. 'Nothing can be done', he said, we can only wait. 'Well, you know', he said, 'it is a communist state'. Well, no, it is not. That is the problem.

Laos is a capitalist country, a closed state locked into neoliberalism. There is, for sure, a history of struggle for communism here, but also a history of tragic failure, failure of a party that modelled itself on the Stalinist communist parties of the Soviet Union and China, and failure in a context of pressure that would have buckled even the most democratic and revolutionary of leaderships.

8

BOLIVARIAN REPUBLIC OF VENEZUELA

The revolutionary baton passed back to Latin America quite unexpectedly right at the end of the twentieth century, posing difficult questions about populism and state power for all of us looking for alternatives now, and especially so in forms of 'socialism' that are in the gift of charismatic leaders who operate in such a way as to make their own version of their so-called socialism operate completely independently of the economy, which remains in the hands of the big capitalists.

This 'República Bolivariana', the 'República Bolivariana de Venezuela', is in the north of the main South American landmass, bounded on the south by Colombia and Brazil and, to the south and east, by a rather fuzzy contested Amazon border with Guyana. Just off the coast to the east is Trinidad and Tobago in the Caribbean. Caracas, the capital, is on the north coast; this is as much a Caribbean as it is a Latin America country.

This is the 'Fifth Republic', named in honour of Simón Bolívar, 'El Libertador' who led the independence struggle against Spain at the beginning of the nineteenth century for what is now Venezuela and Bolivia (and also

Colombia, Ecuador, Peru, and Panama). A Bolivarian republic was declared in a new constitution in 1999 by President Hugo Chávez after his election. Chávez, elected under the rules of the 1961 constitution, convoked a National Constituent Assembly that paved the way for a constitution that was designed to enable wide-ranging changes that were ratified by a referendum soon after. 1999 was, then, a turning point in the history of Venezuela, marking a rapid shift in the balance of power away from the oligarchies that ran the country up to then in what was effectively an oil-producing dependent client-state of the United States.

The question that haunted supporters of Chávez until his death in 2013, and now haunts supporters of his successor Nicolás Maduro, is how far this shift in the balance of power was merely governmental or also economic. The economic factor has always been, of course, a deciding factor in a country marked by huge social divisions between the rich and the poor, between the wealthy inhabitants of parts of the main cities like Caracas, particularly Caracas, and the countryside and barrios which loom up on the mountains that ring the capital city. The middle classes certainly took a hit in the ambitious social programmes that Chávez instituted, but the super-rich have maintained control of the main industries, leading to suspicion that 'socialism' has been a sleight of hand; that there has not been so much an overthrow of the bourgeoisie but a mutation of a radical state apparatus that Chávez managed for a while into a corrupt committee of the 'Boliburgesía'.

What is certain is that whatever concessions Maduro's government makes now will not be enough for a Venezuelan bourgeoisie so closely tied historically to the US, one keen to rake back the privileges it once had before Chávez's election. With the help of the enraged middle class which it mobilises in public demonstrations on the streets against Maduro, the diaspora and local bourgeoisie is intent on destroying this regime. It is intent on ridding the country of any pretension that the 'fifth republic' had to increase literacy and empower the poor, intent on replacing that fifth republic with something a good deal less 'bolivarian'. They are still smarting from erosion of their power, and all the more so by the formation in 2008 of the Partido Socialista Unido de Venezuela, the PSUV, which is now Maduro's power-base.

The process of building an alternative power-base for a revolt against the regime has been by way of economic sabotage and threat of invasion by the US, and hopes of breaking the military, turning it from being Maduro's apparatus into theirs, if necessary through a coup. It is quite understandable that the socialist rhetoric of the regime should be taken at face value by opponents of invasion, but this is to fall into a dangerous trap. Solidarity efforts and socialist movement around the world would thereby be effectively telling lies. Supporters of Chávez and Maduro around the world are willing to overlook all that has gone sour over these last twenty years. But gone sour it has, and mobilisation against sabotage and invasion by imperialism cannot be built on lies. We need to stare the truth in the face.

Before and after Chávez

Before Chávez there was Rafael Caldera, a fairly moderate politician in Venezuelan terms, but 'moderate' in this context meant gearing the economy toward the needs of the United States and turning the state forces against those who disrupted the political-economic project of business as usual in a dependent capitalist country.

Caldera was in power when I first visited the country in 1996 to teach a course at UCV, the Universidad Central de Venezuela, where Caldera himself had studied law and political science. UCV was a fairly liberal institution that operated as a resource-base for many of those who resisted the Caldera regime, and was home to radical academic groups influenced by liberation theology who were willing to work with communities in the barrios. People from these communities would sometimes turn up at UCV buildings and ask for help, and I was shown details of one housing project being set up in response to a demand for help, set up by staff in the architecture department.

Those communities in the barrios had risen up, or, rather, flooded down into downtown Caracas in February 1989 during what was known as 'El Caracazo'. The government had implemented austerity policies demanded by the International Monetary Fund. The diverse legacies of that movement were to be found among supporters of Chávez in his own 1992 coup attempt against the regime before he was eventually elected, an indication of his mass popular support, particularly among the poor. Chávez had already set up the Movimiento Bolivariano Revolucionario 200, MBR-200, which planned that failed coup, and it was this organisation that was to become the Movement for the Fifth Republic in 1997 to support his candidacy in the 1998 presidential election. Resistance was therefore brewing in the widespread discontent with the regime in 1996, but the US and their local aides were still very much in power.

In the hotel where I was staying in Chacao in the centre of Caracas, a big oil-industry guy from Texas told me that he could show me how to make big money. He was in his late fifties maybe and his check shirt struggled to cover his belly. His hair was slicked back over skin that looked like beaten leather. His fingernails curved around the tips of hands that he clapped together above his head as he shouted to the waiter, 'Boy!' He wore sunglasses at breakfast, and told me that people would do anything for you in this place if you asked them right; they were liable to be lazy and so you had had to tell them what to do. 'Yes', he said, 'there is money to be made here', 'it's here for the taking', and, 'if you're interested, I can show you how it's done'. I tried to avoid him, and was thankful he wasn't there during the second week of my stay when I came back to Caracas after a weekend away in Canaima, back for the second week of teaching.

The teaching was in a tower block a metro-ride away from the hotel, and the School of Psychology of the Universidad Central de Venezuela was accessed through a shopping complex on the ground floor. That's where we went for a coffee during the breaks, so many kinds of coffee. Most-times I was collected from my hotel and ferried to UCV; when I made my way there one time by metro and walked from the station to the department the teaching staff who had arranged the course I was teaching on were horrified. I was warned time and again that the city was violent, including the area around the department.

It was a city built on oil, and the car was king, choking the urban centres and making walking hazardous. The district mayor of Chacao, where I was staying, was Irene Sáez who had been Miss Universe in 1981; she equipped the police on traffic duty with white gloves, a sign of what a nice clean and safe place it was in contrast to other parts of the city. It was cute, and treated as a bit of joke by my hosts. Irene Sáez is not to be confused with the 1996 winner, Alicia Machado, who was weight-shamed by Trump in 1996 and who became a progressive activist; Sáez was anything but.

The senior professors in UCV were formally retired – the salaries and pension-age of academic personnel having been linked to that of the military in a concession wrought from the regime a few years before – and this meant that it was difficult for junior teaching staff to get permanent contracts and then promotion. It was a paradox, and one of the contradictions of UCV in relation to the regime, that these liberal voices in community-support initiatives in the barrios needed the university as a base, but also then effectively enabled the institution to run at a very low-cost. These radical academics were subsidising the university. Some well-heeled well-meaning 'community psychologists' delivered free medicines to the barrios in their Mercedes. The university was being run down, and the email ran very slow.

Teaching was in the mornings, but one day we broke early to take to the streets in a demonstration that began at UCV and made its way in the hot sun to the Palacio de Miraflores, centre of government. This was to protest at the crackdown by the police and army against previous demonstrations that were in support of those still being harassed and arrested following the Caracazo and the MBR-200 coup attempt. Our section of the march against police violence chanted for UCV as one of the emblems of the resistance, with two main slogans; one was 'U. U. U.C.V.', and the other was 'Por qué por qué por qué nos asesinan, si somos el future de América Latina' ('why do they kill us if we are the future of Latin America?').

The threats were external and obvious, and part of a tense coexistence deal brokered with the regime was that the security forces not be allowed to enter the university campus. There were similar arrangements between the regime and universities in other Latin American countries. The threats were also, more worryingly, internal and implicit, provoking some paranoia inside the university; there was speculation about the real identity of apparently ultra-left protesters, the 'encapuchados' – 'the masked ones' – who appeared on the edges of the campus, destroying property and then vanishing. I was told variously that they were leftists infiltrated by the regime, criminal gangs and outright provocateurs.

Colombians were also, I was told by nice liberal junior members of staff in the department, 'untrustworthy'. This was because they were more likely to be poor, immigrants working as domestic helps, which seemed to be the case in the anecdotes told me in Caracas. In Parque Nacional de

Canaima in the Amazon near the border with Brazil and Guyana I shared a cabin with a wealthy Colombian family just over for vacation and a visit to Salto Ángel, the world's longest uninterrupted waterfall. The 'tepui' high table mountains each had their own micro-climates and isolated species, inspiration for Conan Doyle's 1912 novel *The Lost World*. The Colombians dressed well, perhaps a little inappropriately for jungle treks. Our local guide, Venezuelan, nudged me one day and pointed to them as we navigated a walk alongside a waterfall, whispering in a mixture of awe, disparagement and suspicion, 'they really are stars aren't they!'.

One of the students attending the course was Isabel Rodríguez Mora who I had seen briefly a couple of years before at a conference in Santiago de Chile, striding across the stage to receive an award for best undergraduate thesis. Her research was on community mobilization and repression. It was a dangerous topic and her supervisors were already worried about what might happen to her. She interviewed me for a local newsletter.

A few months after I left Caracas, Isabel was arrested, and an international campaign against her detention was conducted among psychologists and other academics. She was released from prison in January 1997, and managed to get out of Venezuela to do post-graduate research soon after. Isabel and her supervisor Maritza Montero were my main points of contact immediately after my first visit, mainly because they travelled abroad more often and relatively easily, and it was through them that I heard about the election of Chávez the following year, and about their hopes and doubts.

Hugo Chávez in power

It was unclear whether Chávez would become president in 1998, but he was a popular voice for the poor, and the right was hopelessly divided. Irene Sáez, mayor of Chacao district, spent millions on publicity as an 'independent' candidate, but dropped out after rapid falls in the polls earlier in the year. By the time I returned for my second visit to Venezuela in June 1999, Chávez had been installed in the Palacio de Miraflores and had seen through the radical constitutional changes he had promised during his campaign.

The Sociedad Interamericana de Psicología congress at the Caracas Hilton, a biennial meeting for émigrés to return home and meet friends and go shopping as well as functioning as a contact point for some radicals, seemed to be trying hard not to speak about the new president or the new political situation. The congress site moves around Latin America amid much bureaucratic and political palaver, the society itself having been set up with US-American finance and agendas after the Second World War. A prominent US-American visiting speaker was mugged on his way to the hotel from the airport, but no one could blame Chávez for that.

The liberals and radicals in UCV were also divided. Isabel Rodríguez Mora was already joking that Chávez was a bit crazy, but perhaps better than the previous regime, though her mother was more critical. A third position was already beginning to emerge, that of the self-declared 'Ni-Nis', those who said no to Chávez and no to the right-wing opposition that was beginning to flex its muscles. 'Look, this is a third world country', said Isabel, pointing to the immense difficulties any radical regime would have in dealing with the massive inequalities and the determination of those with privileges to hold onto them.

It was already clear that if Chávez was to succeed, then that would have to involve taking big business interests into public ownership and, crucially, preventing the reprivatisation of the state oil company Petróleos de Venezuela S. A., PDVSA, which was already on the cards before his election as president, and which the right-wing had their eyes on as a main prize and as a sign to the United States that they were moving things in the right direction. Venezuela was then the fifth largest exporter of oil to the rest of the world, and the fourth largest supplier of oil to the US. PDVSA was a massive enterprise operating effectively as a separate state apparatus able to circumvent extraction laws, and although it had been formally nationalised in 1976, it operated in tandem with US oil interests, managed by a US-friendly team. The 1999 Constitution, which was drawn up after assemblies that included indigenous peoples affected by extractive mining, prohibited the reprivatisation of PDVSA, and Chávez began to appoint a new management board so that he could then push for an increase in oil prices in OPEC to fund reforms.

Oil was to become the financial power-base for the new regime, but this natural resource also paved the way for a new twist on the clientalist mechanisms already entrenched in the Venezuelan state; instead of PDVSA and the President awarding kickbacks to loyal cronies, Chávez was able to himself bypass bureaucratic mechanisms and reach beyond them, below them, to deal with popular grievances. This was one of the sources of his popularity even then, that he would move fast and address popular complaints about lack of services; it had the predictable effect of reinforcing his personal power, fuelling the worries of liberals (and not only bad-faith bad liberals), those concerned with democratic procedures.

I urgently needed antibiotics during my visit in 1999 which Isabel took me to collect from under the almost closed shutters of a chemist, without a prescription and beyond their sell-by date. We travelled together to Colonia Tovar, a once isolated old German enclave dating from the mid-nineteenth century about forty miles from Caracas where you could eat the local strawberries in rolling green hills and Swiss-style chalets. A paved road led out of the edge of Caracas, a poor part of town which was shrouded on either side with tangles of illegal electricity and telephone wires trailing their way to shacks and shops.

By the time I got back to Caracas for my third visit, in September 2010, the division between the right-wing opposition and leftist 'Chavista' supporters of the regime had widened, and the space for the Ni-Nis all but closed down, though some of my friends there still held that 'third' position. Now Chávez had been in power for over ten years, and reports from visitors were mixed, as you would expect. During those ten years we had visits from Venezuelan students and friends and relatives of friends who would range in their opinions of Chávez from grudging admiration to outright hostility. The daughter and son-in-law of one of the professors at UCV came to dinner one evening, and things went well until we asked 'What about Chávez?'; all hell broke loose, almost a civil war in the kitchen in a raging argument between the two of them.

The 'community' activists in UCV were, apparently, most put out by the arrival in the barrios of Cuban medical teams who were effectively replacing the charitable work-teams that had been sent there on research visits and student-placement. The 'oil for doctors' scheme had begun shortly after a disastrous mud-slide on the outskirts of Caracas that killed 20,000 people, a catastrophe and humanitarian intervention that was research topic of Isabel Rodriguez Mora's PhD from her new émigré base in Cambridge. Under the scheme Cuba provided Venezuela with around 31,000 medical personnel and training, and in exchange Venezuela handed over 100,000 barrels of oil a day. So, Chávez was unpopular with some of the UCV folk on two counts; he was rendering unnecessary those already working in the barrios and he was giving oil to another country. These complaints were sometimes tinged with national chauvinism, if not racism.

Isabel wrote about the way that political conflicts in Venezuela were increasingly polarised not only around class – poor districts of the city against the wealthier suburbs – but around race. She described, in an article that was overall critical of Chávez, the way that street protests for and against the regime were being 'feminised', mobilising feminist arguments, and she noted how the Chavistas were racialised; this was not only in representations of them as poorer and more likely to be black but also on the streets in reality. The anti-Chávez mobilisations were overwhelmingly in richer whiter neighbourhoods.

Radical academic work was closing down at UCV by 2010, with professors who staffed the courses for free, really retiring from work there altogether, or emigrating. A special issue of *Journal of Prevention and Intervention in the Community* edited by Maritza Montero in 2004, for example, had bizarrely barely mentioned Chávez. It was as if they could not bear to think about it, and would rather pretend that the Bolivarian revolution did not exist.

During this 2010 visit I stayed with and was ferried around by academic colleagues who were, by now, hostile to the regime. I gave a talk on 'critical psychology' at the private Universidad Católica Andrés Bello, and was told afterwards that I 'sounded like a Chavista'. I must admit that every unfair whining petty complaint about Chávez during this visit made me more sympathetic to him. We would walk past a state-owned 'Abasto Bicentenario' supermarket that provided low-cost goods for poor people, for example, and be told that this was simply a 'stunt' that benefitted no-one and that anyone with any sense would not shop there anyway.

Parliamentary elections were taking place, and quite important ones since the previous parliamentary elections held in 2005 were boycotted by the opposition. This time they were standing as the Mesa de la Unidad Democrática, MUD, up against Chávez's Partido Socialista Unido de Venezuela, PSUV. Our hosts were going to vote for the MUD. So, we were repeatedly told that Chávez was undemocratic and that there were no free and fair elections, and then taken to the polling station. It was in a quite posh area, and white parents in white linen suits left their kids in air-conditioned cars to line up outside and wait to vote.

It was difficult to get out of the country this time. Well, this because of the traffic which clogged the chaotic streets leading to the airport. We just made it. Two colleagues who had retired from UCV drove us while checking with Twitter every minute for details of road-jams, warning us that you cannot trust the radio reports. This was the dominant mode of avoidance and engagement; distrust of anything the government said or did. The liberals complained, and the right accused Chávez of being a communist, something he steadfastly denied. He was a populist who used socialist rhetoric that frightened a lot of people, but his economic policies were not even socialist. At the highpoint of the nationalisation process, just before Chávez's death in 2013, the right-wing press and Venezuelan big business were squealing about the actually still very limited encroachments on their property and power.

After Chávez

If Chávez was bad, we were told, Nicolás Maduro who was elected president in 2013 after Chávez died was worse. Chávez looked like a 'mestizo', not fully white, one crime in the eyes of opponents, and came from a middle-class family and so obviously a hypocrite, a double crime. Maduro, a bus-driver, was obviously not suited for office in their eyes. At one of the SIP conferences I was informed by a professor who was still at UCV that Maduro was 'really Colombian'. The election was contested, then the result was contested, and the right has not let up since in a propaganda war and then a campaign of economic sabotage in which the large companies, still in private hands, have restricted the supply of basic goods and then blamed the government for shortages. The problem is that Maduro is a hopeless populist, little more than a caudillo.

The opposition has staged provocations on the streets, and there have been deaths on both sides, with the 2017 clashes operating as a dress rehearsal for a full-scale revolt and perhaps a coup. The Maduro government has responded by tightening security, and, driven ahead with extractive mining projects in indigenous land areas, something that has enabled the right to recruit new supporters from among the dispossessed. The very allies that the regime needs are being alienated in the process, and the ecological dimension of any possible socialist transformation in Venezuela is under threat.

These contradictions were already pointed out in two of the best guides to the process unrolling in Venezuela; the 2008 survey of the promise and shortcomings of the revolution, *The Real Venezuela*, by Iain Bruce in 2008, and the 2010 collection *Venezuela Speaks! Voices from the Grassroots* edited by Carlos Martinez, Michael Fox and Jojo Farrell. Meanwhile things get worse and worse, politically and economically.

There was a report in June 2019, to the delight of the opposition, that the last store in the government-owned Abastos Bicentenario supermarket chain had closed. Each and every contradiction discussed by Bruce in *The Real Venezuela* and noted in the accounts collected together in *Venezuela Speaks!* is intensified.

The human rights situation in Venezuela is now very grim, with Amnesty International noting a series of systematic abuses of power, ranging from attacks on protesters to extra-judicial killings by the regime. The fact that Juan Guiadó's supporters are also clearly willing to resort to violence, including in the April 2020 botched 'invasion' by mercenaries linked to the US, is not an excuse for this. The regime's response merely makes it easier for the opposition to recruit the poor who are under increasing pressure as Maduro imposes austerity measures.

Left solidarity and critique

The most recent face-to-face discussion I had with friends from Venezuela was with two political comrades from opposing organisations that were, in different ways, still Trotskyist. I have to say, though I am reluctant to admit it here, that the anti-Chavista comrade was leaner, taller and whiter than the more obviously working-class supporter of the regime. Stereotypes have a basis in reality and play back into the political debates. One of the comrades was a member of LUCHAS, which still operates as a critical left voice of the Maduro regime, and tries to participate in the PSUV and the government controlled trades unions, though with increasing difficulty. Expressed loyalty to the Bolivarian revolution is not enough; any criticism is taken as a sign of secret allegiance to the right-wing opposition. LUCHAS will not save itself because of its name, the 'Liga

Unitaria Chavista Socialista'. LUCHAS had split from Marea Socialista which the other comrade was still a member of.

Marea Socialista has a much more explicitly critical perspective on the Maduro regime. The row between members of the two groups was specifically over the agreement of representatives of Marea Socialista to participate in talks with Juan Guaidó. Guaidó was educated at Universidad Católica Andrés Bello and George Washington University, former member of the MUD and clearly a place-holder for US interests. Marea Socialista insisted that they had made no concessions in these talks and had been clear about their position, which was to defend every gain of the Bolivarian revolution, but it was a bad move. LUCHAS was, understandably, incandescent while Marea Socialista indignantly demanded acknowledgement of the censorship of one of the few platforms of dissent inside Venezuela, the Aporrea.org site.

It is clear that Guaidó is a willing agent of the US, and will implement a Chilean-style dictatorship-bloodbath 'solution' to the situation in Venezuela. Nicolás Maduro is not Salvador Allende, though, and he has himself worsened the conditions in the country, setting in place the very pre-conditions for a coup. The strengthening of the armed forces is designed to protect the state from external attack, but a successful coup will itself rely on key elements of the army coming over to the opposition and placing their bets on Guaidó. Both LUCHAS and Marea Socialista issued statements condemning the attempted coup in April 2019, both published on the website of the

Fourth International, an organisation that was still desperately trying to maintain comradely working relations between two groups of revolutionary socialist activists who have taken different paths through the tangled reality of Venezuelan pretend-socialism.

Disappointingly, but understandably, Marea Socialista felt betrayed by the Fourth International's support for LUCHAS, and so, in late 2019, they linked up with the International Socialist League which has a better position on Venezuela. The response by LUCHAS to the COVID-19 crisis has included abject praise for the regime's handling of the crisis and a craven response and appeal to Maduro to listen to his old compañeros and build socialism, some hope. The future of human rights and the possibility of any socialist renewal, redeeming the promise of the Bolivarian revolution, will depend on the left groups working together at this time of crisis while speaking out against the abuses of power that prepare the way for dictatorship.

Apart from the internal problems, the external policies of Chávez and then Maduro have been disastrous, them allying with despotic regimes around the world, ranging from Mugabe in Zimbabwe to Assad in Syria, and all with the hope of impressing a new possible client interest in China or Russia, not to mention their toxic 'solidarity' with the Palestinians that has slid from critique of Zionism at times into antisemitic rhetoric. Attempts by Chávez to woo Putin did succeed to some extent, requiring some diplomatic manoeuvres to show loyalty to other corrupt capitalist regimes around the world that were sucking up to Russia, but it was always clear that Russia was playing a strategic geo-political game and would have any ally in power in Venezuela that would be compliant. Pragmatics, as always, overrides political principles for Russia, and in May 2020 Rosneft, the country's biggest oil producer, pulled the plugs on Maduro. China has been keen to move into Venezuela as another willing client state. The process of economic alignment begun under Chávez has been ramped up by Maduro, and Venezuela is now China's biggest investment opportunity in Latin America. However, China too has been playing cat and mouse with Maduro, closing contracts and then seeing rich pickings in the COVID-19 crisis, yet further evidence that neither regime can be considered to be socialist.

Foreign policy is in the service of economic trade deals that worsen the grip of private enterprise on the country, something that has never really been tackled, a deadly mistake, and this cynical foreign policy agenda is then parroted by sympathetic media outlets like Telesur which was set up by Chávez with its headquarters in Caracas. From there come reports of the demonstrations against the regime in Nicaragua which are systematically skewed in favour of the Ortega government. This makes it all the more difficult to mount campaigns against imperialist intervention. With friends like that, activists ask, what kinds of friends are these?

Here you have to remember what the campist project is. It is one thing to support socialist regimes, or regimes moving to socialise the means of production and distribution, against attack, but it is quite another to pretend that regimes that are not at all socialist are fully on our side. Campism wipes away these differences on the assumption that there are only two great 'camps' or blocs in the world, and that if one of them is progressive, oriented to Russia, say, or China, then every regime allied with that bloc is also portrayed as progressive, must be treated as our friend, must be let off the hook and, when it comes down to it, have crimes hidden from view in order to build solidarity with it.

Some campists who had previously overlooked problems with the regime have recently thought better of it, citing a number of reasons for their disillusionment, which include the failure to escape from the 'oil extraction' trap; that is, that Chávez relied for his success on being able to give handouts to the poor using oil money which relies on the despoliation of the environment. The Orinoco Mineral Mining Arc project is the last straw for many ecosocialists who have previously been tempted to fall in line with the Maduro regime. This oil extraction trap is something that fed the populist character of Chávez and then Maduro, who has seen his popularity fall. The relentless destabilisation campaign from outside Venezuela has then been able to key into popular discontent. These are the key contradictions of a project that was always 'top down', something that even sympathetic commentators noted.

It should be remembered that while the 1999 Bolivarian Constitution prevented the reprivatisation of the state oil company, PDVSA, the company continued to operate as if it was a private enterprise, fulfilling the regime's agenda in a weird kind of public-private partnership that never took power away from big business and the large property owners. Despite the name sometimes given to this Bolivarian project, and despite the name of Chávez's own political party, this was never a socialist country.

The Bolivarian revolution was at the head of the so-called 'pink tide' in Latin America. After the election of Chávez we saw Lula elected in Brazil in 2003 and then Evo Morales in Bolivia three years later. Imperialism and its local agents are now on the offensive, but we need to know who is a friend and who is a liability. We need to be clear what we are defending when we defend a regime from imperialist attack, and so we have to be clear that a big part of the problem is precisely the enemy, the bourgeoisie, at home, at home in Venezuela itself.

There was a serious promise of socialism in Venezuela, but of a type that needs to be located in the context of military and populist leaderships in Latin America that have always been more concerned about their own charismatic authority than with the construction of entirely new forms of power in the hands of those who produce the wealth. Blueprints imposed from above disconnected from economic transformation cannot ever be socialist, a lesson that has been drummed home over the past century since October 1917.

BIBLIOGRAPHY

Bruce, I. (2008) *The Real Venezuela: Making Socialism in the 21st Century*. London: Pluto Books.

Engels, F. (1884) *The Origin of the Family, Private Property and the State*, available online at:
https://www.marxists.org/archive/marx/works/1884/origin-family/index.htm

Evans, G. (2012) *A Short History of Laos: The Land in Between*. Chaing Mai, Thailand: Silkworm Books.

Hobsbawm, E. and Ranger, T. (Eds) (1983) *The Invention of Tradition*. Cambridge: Cambridge University Press.

Kautsky, K. (1921) *Georgia: A Social-Democratic Peasant Republic – Impressions and Observations*, available online at:
https://www.marxists.org/archive/kautsky/1921/georgia/index.htm

Kim, S. (2013) *Everyday Life in the North Korean Revolution, 1945-1950*. Ithaca, NY: Cornell University Press.

Kim, S. (2014) *Without You There Is No Us: My Time with the Sons of North Korea's Elite*. New York: Crown Publishing.

Lee, E. (2017) *The Experiment: Georgia's Forgotten Revolution 1918-1921*. London: Zed Books.

Lister, J. (1985) *Cuba: Radical Face of Stalinism*, available online at:
https://www.marxists.org/history/etol/document/wsl/lister/cuba-lister85.htm

Loong-Yu, A. (2012) *China's Rise: Strength and Fragility*. London: Resistance Books.

Maitan, L. (1976) Party, Army and Masses in China: *A Marxist Interpretation of the Cultural Revolution and Its Aftermath*. London: New Left Books.

Mandel, E. (1985) *Dictatorship of the Proletariat and Socialist Democracy*, available online at: https://www.marxists.org/archive/mandel/1985/dictprole/1985.htm

Mandel, E. (1992) *Power and Money: A Marxist Theory of Bureaucracy*. London: Verso.

Martinez, C., Fox, M. and Farrell, J. (Eds) (2010) *Venezuela Speaks! Voices from the Grassroots*. Oakland, CA: PM Press.

Marx, K. (1875) *Critique of the Gotha Programme*, available online at: https://www.marxists.org/archive/marx/works/1875/gotha/

Marx, K. and Engels, F. (1948) *Manifesto of the Communist Party*, online at: https://www.marxists.org/archive/marx/works/1848/communist-manifesto/

Murphy, D. (2001) *One Foot in Laos*. New York: Overlook Press.

Murphy, D. (2010) *The Island That Dared: Journeys in Cuba*. London: Eland Publishing.

Musić, G. (2013) *Serbia's Working Class in Transition 1988-2013*, available online at: https://arhiv.rosalux.rs/en/artikl.php?id=262

Pomerantsev, P. (2014) *Nothing is True and Everything is Possible: Adventures in Modern Russia*. New York: PublicAffairs.

Radenković, I. (2016) *Foreign Direct Investments in Serbia*, available online at: https://www.rosalux.rs/en/foreign-direct-investments-serbia

Samary, C. and Leplat, F. (Eds) (2019) *Decolonial Communism, Democracy and the Commons*. London: Resistance Books and Amsterdam: IIRE.

Trotsky, L. (1905) *The Permanent Revolution & Results and Prospects,* available online at:
https://www.marxists.org/archive/trotsky/1931/tpr/index.ht
m

Trotsky, L. (1922) *Between Red and White: A Study of Some Fundamental Questions of Revolution, With Particular Relevance to Georgia,* available online at:
https://www.marxists.org/archive/trotsky/1922/red-white/index.htm

Trotsky, L. (1932) *The History of the Russian Revolution,* available online at:
https://www.marxists.org/archive/trotsky/1930/hrr/

Trotsky, L. (1937) *The Revolution Betrayed: What is the Soviet Union and Where is it Going?,* available online at:
https://www.marxists.org/archive/trotsky/1936/revbet/inde
x.htm

Trotsky, L. (1938) *The Death Agony of Capitalism and the Tasks of the Fourth International,* available online at:
https://www.marxists.org/archive/trotsky/1938/tp/

Wang Fan-hsi (1991) *Wang Fan-hsi: Chinese Revolutionary, Memoirs 1919-1949.* New York: Columbia University Press.

Wood, T. (2018) *Russia Without Putin: Money, Power and the Myths of the New Cold War.* London: Verso.

About Resistance Books and the IIRE

Resistance Books is the publishing arm of Socialist Resistance. We publish books independently, and also jointly with Merlin Press (London) and the International Institute for Research and Education (Amsterdam). Further information about Resistance Books, including a full list of titles available and how to order them, can be obtained at www.resistancebooks.org.

To contact Resistance Books:
> Email: info@resistancebooks.org
> Website: www.resistancebooks.org
> Post: Resistance Books, PO Box 62732, London, SW2 9GQ.

Socialist Resistance is a revolutionary Marxist, internationalist, ecosocialist and feminist political network. Analysis and news from Socialist Resistance can be read online at www.socialistresistance.org

Socialist Resistance collaborates with the Fourth International, whose online magazine, *International Viewpoint*, can be viewed at: www.internationalviewpoint.org

The International Institute for Research and Education is a centre for the development of critical thought and the exchange of experiences and ideas between people engaged in their struggles. Since 1982, when the Institute opened in Amsterdam, its main activity has been the organisation of courses for progressive forces around the world. The seminars, courses and study groups deal with all subjects related to the emancipation of the oppressed and exploited around the world. It has welcomed participants from across the world, most of them from developing countries. The IIRE provides activists and academics opportunities for research and education in three locations: Amsterdam, Islamabad and Manila.

The IIRE publishes *Notebooks for Study and Research*, which focus on contemporary political debates, as well as themes of historical and theoretical importance. The *Notebooks* have appeared in several languages besides English and French. All the *Notebooks* are available by going to http://iire.org/en/resources/notebooks-for-study-and-research.html. Other publications and audio files of the events held at the IIRE are available in several languages and can be freely downloaded from www.iire.org

To contact the International Institute for Research and Education:
Email: iire@iire.org
Website: www.iire.org
Phone: 00 31 20 671 7263
Post: International Institute for Research and Education, Lombokstraat 40, Amsterdam, 1094 AL, The Netherlands